EVERYTHING You Need to Know About ASSET ALLOCATION

How To Balance Risk & Reward to Make it Work for Your Investments

ALAN NORTHCOTT

Everything You Need to Know About Asset Allocation: How To Balance Risk & Reward to Make it Work for Your Investments

1405 SW 6th Ave. • Ocala, Florida 34471
Phone: 800-814-1132 • Fax: 352-622-1875
Website: www.atlantic-pub.com • E-mail: sales@atlantic-pub.com
SAN Number: 268-1250

Northcott, Alan, 1951-
Everything you need to know about asset allocation : how to balance risk & reward to make it work for your investments / by Alan Northcott.
p. cm.
Includes bibliographical references and index.
ISBN-13: 978-1-60138-322-8 (alk. paper)
ISBN-10: 1-60138-322-3 (alk. paper)
1. Asset allocation. 2. Portfolio management. 3. Investments. 4. Asset allocation--Case studies. 5. Portfolio management--Case studies. I. Title.
HG4529.5.N67 2011
332.63'2--dc22

2011002158

BOOK PRODUCTION DESIGN: T.L. Price • design@tlpricefreelance.com

Printed in the United States

A few years back we lost our beloved pet dog Bear, who was not only our best and dearest friend but also the "Vice President of Sunshine" here at Atlantic Publishing. He did not receive a salary but worked tirelessly 24 hours a day to please his parents.

Bear was a rescue dog who turned around and showered myself, my wife, Sherri, his grandparents Jean, Bob, and Nancy, and every person and animal he met (well, maybe not rabbits) with friendship and love. He made a lot of people smile every day.

We wanted you to know a portion of the profits of this book will be donated in Bear's memory to local animal shelters, parks, conservation organizations, and other individuals and nonprofit organizations in need of assistance.

– Douglas & Sherri Brown

PS: We have since adopted two more rescue dogs: first Scout, and the following year, Ginger. They were both mixed golden retrievers who needed a home.

Want to help animals and the world? Here are a dozen easy suggestions you and your family can implement today:

- *Adopt and rescue a pet from a local shelter.*
- *Support local and no-kill animal shelters.*
- *Plant a tree to honor someone you love.*
- *Be a developer — put up some birdhouses.*
- *Buy live, potted Christmas trees and replant them.*
- *Make sure you spend time with your animals each day.*
- *Save natural resources by recycling and buying recycled products.*
- *Drink tap water, or filter your own water at home.*
- *Whenever possible, limit your use of or do not use pesticides.*
- *If you eat seafood, make sustainable choices.*
- *Support your local farmers market.*
- *Get outside. Visit a park, volunteer, walk your dog, or ride your bike.*

Five years ago, Atlantic Publishing signed the Green Press Initiative. These guidelines promote environmentally friendly practices, such as using recycled stock and vegetable-based inks, avoiding waste, choosing energy-efficient resources, and promoting a no-pulping policy. We now use 100-percent recycled stock on all our books. The results: in one year, switching to post-consumer recycled stock saved 24 mature trees, 5,000 gallons of water, the equivalent of the total energy used for one home in a year, and the equivalent of the greenhouse gases from one car driven for a year.

Dedication

Dedicated to my beautiful wife, Liz, my constant companion through life's adventures and strength for more than 30 years.

With special thanks to Melissa Peterson at Atlantic Publishing, the editor of many of my books, and to Doug Brown, the publisher, who shares my love of and concern for animals.

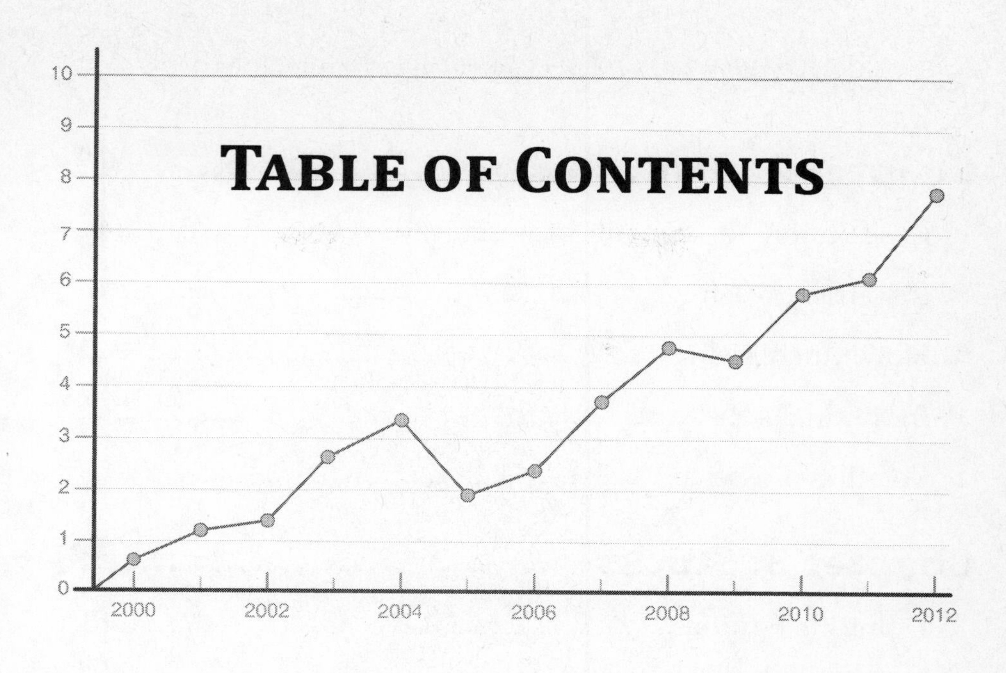

TABLE OF CONTENTS

7
8
9
4
5
M–
M+
CE
%

INTRODUCTION

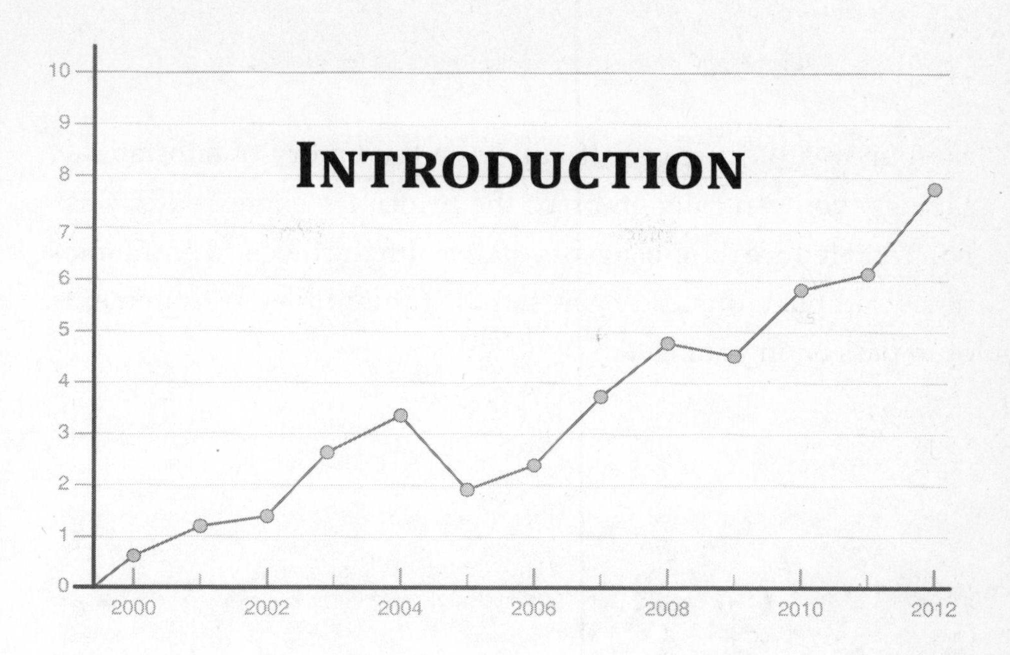

IF YOU HAVE ANY SAVINGS OR INVESTMENTS, ASSET allocation is something you must learn about. It does not matter how large or how small your investments are, any portfolio can benefit from applying the lessons of asset allocation. You will learn from reading this book that asset allocation can, almost by magic, reduce the risk to your wealth while increasing the returns, and although this seems hard to believe, it is one reason becoming conversant with asset allocation is so essential.

You might be a new investor with only one or two investments in your portfolio, but learning how to choose those investments and develop your portfolio will still benefit your account. You might come to investing through contributing to an employer-offered 401(k) plan or having savings bonds in your name your parents or relatives bought when you were a child. If either is the case, you will benefit from planning how to progress with your portfolio as your wealth increases. If you have the luxury of substantial savings, you can fully embrace the principles expressed in this book and reduce the erosion of your wealth during hard economic times and plan for steady gains in the future for your retirement or to pass on in your estate.

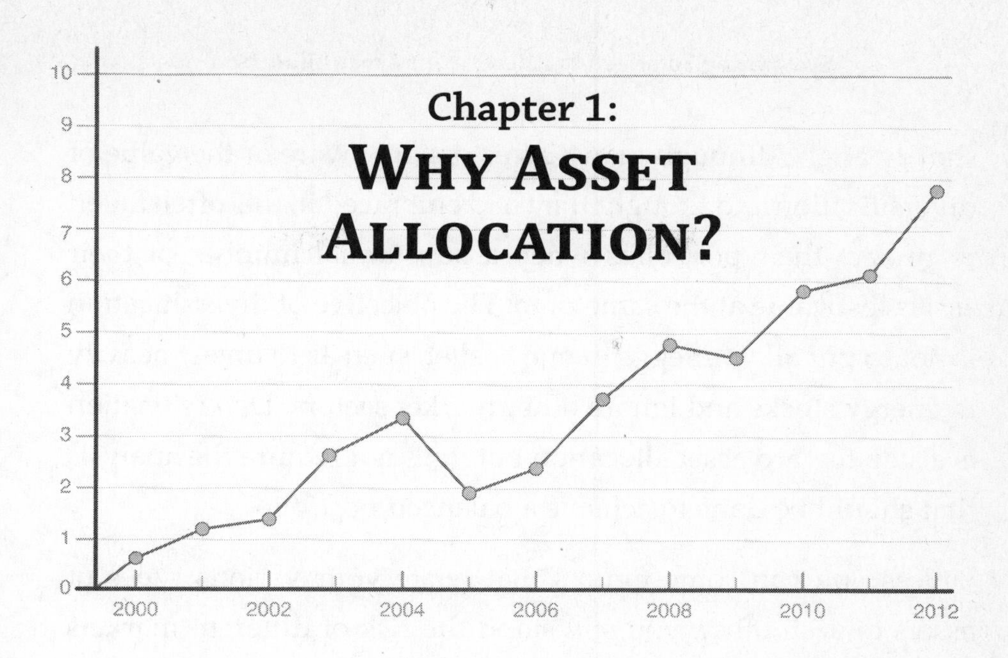

Chapter 1: Why Asset Allocation?

THE FIRST BIG INVESTMENT FOR MANY OF PEOPLE IS their home. In the past, this was considered the best way to keep and increase the value of your money. The view that you could not go wrong with investing in real estate was severely tested during the early 2000s, and thus has caused many people to question whether they can retain and improve their wealth regardless of the markets. Asset allocation plays a key role in this because it quantifies the risks and rewards of different ways of using your money. Real estate is only one category outside the financial markets you can consider to be part of your asset allocation plan. *Chapter 5 looks at alternative ways you can invest in real estate that can make sense in conjunction with a financial portfolio.*

Just as many people learned a lesson about the housing market a decade ago, a warning about investing in financial markets came shortly after. Although many investors are aware of the value of diversification and thought they had embraced it, this often failed to protect their portfolios when a substantial number of their assets lost value at the same time. The objective of diversification is not to put all your eggs in one basket, such as to invest heavily in energy stocks and ignore other market sectors. Diversification is a step toward asset allocation but does not require the analysis that should be done to achieve a balanced portfolio.

Unless you run some figures that relate your various types of assets to each other, you still stand the risk of different markets pulling each other down. Asset allocation might not give you a perfect solution to this, but it does recognize the shortcomings of simple diversification. It will give your portfolio more protection if it is applied and regularly checked when circumstances and investments change.

One of the wisdoms of the financial markets was that there were two ways to approach keeping and making money. For those who took an active interest in their finances, there was the option to learn about trading, or buying and selling stocks and other financial securities and trying to choose those that would increase their value in days, weeks, or months at most. The study of technical analysis, which started about 100 years ago with Charles Dow, facilitated this. But this is a technically and emotionally difficult pursuit. Trading tempts many people who think that is where money is made, but without adequate preparation and education, 90 percent of traders fail within the first six months.

The other approach was buying and holding investments long term and ignoring the daily fluctuations with the idea that this was the way to increase your wealth over time. Many believed this would always work just as many believed house prices could never fall. The investments were selected using fundamental analysis, a way to drill down through the figures to determine the underlying value of a particular company in terms of its present and future returns. The overriding principle was that the value might not be realized in this month or the next, but the value was real, and the markets would inevitably recognize this. Unfortunately, the principle that markets will always increase and provide good returns in a reasonable number of years has been challenged. Using centuries as a time frame for the investments would perhaps still work, but the fluctuations have proven too massive for this to continue to be considered a safe course for retirement savings.

Many economists came to the conclusion asset allocation was not the answer to avoiding risk because it failed countless people six years ago.. This might have been because of the confusion over diversification, which was not beneficial when so many markets lost value in 2008. However, growth has helped the stock market replenish itself. Below is a list of growth for the following stock market companies:

S&P 500	+29.6%
MSCI (Europe, Asia, Australia)	+15%
MSCI (emerging markets)	+0.7%
Real Estate Investment Trusts	+28%
High Yield Bonds	+13.6%
Commodities	+22%

In the past, investors and their financial advisors fully believed their portfolios were secure against falling values because they contained a calculated blend of stocks; bonds; commodities; real estate; and international investments, including emerging markets. Many people did not foresee that the financial markets as a whole could fall so dramatically.

The significant losses caused advisors and economists to return to the drawing board to find new and better ways to ensure portfolios could be insulated from significant risks. The lesson learned was there is more to establishing a correct asset allocation plan than what had previously been applied: buying, allocating, and holding financial instruments. The dramatic downturn in the markets showed advisors and investors the importance of tracking market conditions and trends. You cannot choose a perfect allocation model and sit back until retirement or until the funds are needed. Asset allocation is an ongoing process, and although 2008 was an exceptional year, keeping track of portfolios and making adjustments whenever circumstances require are necessary.

Quite a few advisors told their clients they should just wait out the fluctuations, not rush to sell, and the market would recover. These advisors had to admit this strategy was inadequate. Depending on the advice they listened to, some of those investors who were attempting to balance their portfolios on their own without the assistance of a professional suddenly wished they had someone who could give them investment advice. Whether this would have been any better than their own instincts is debatable.

The outcome of 2008 is investors learned they need to make changes in their asset allocation more often than they thought. Investors who thought an annual review of their portfolio was adequate are now looking at monthly reviews or better. This has been a tough lesson to learn, and the financial industry has emerged with a new outlook.

Buying, allocating, and holding onto investments is now proven to be a flawed strategy that cannot avoid losses in the event of a market crash. When applying asset allocation and looking at the future potential of the market, rely on previous historical data and consider current market conditions and trends. Don't just rely on past performance to predict future results.

Key to Asset Allocation

Asset allocation can go against the odds and provide you with more security for your financial portfolio. The key to this is selecting a number of asset classes that will work together to reduce the risk. The process of building a portfolio involves finding investments that do not fluctuate in concert with each other or which have a negative relationship, so when one goes down, the other goes up.

An example of this on a small scale would be airline shares and stocks in an oil company. If the price of oil went up, the oil company shares would tend to increase in value. At the same time, increasing fuel costs would have a negative impact on airline profitability and therefore on the price of those shares. The opposite is also true. If oil prices decreased, airlines would be more easily able to make a profit, and their shares should go up when oil companies would be struggling.

It is possible the markets could go down as a whole, which happened in the past, and holding stocks in both the airlines and oil companies would not mitigate that risk. The simple example above demonstrates there are ways in which it is possible to reduce risk with careful selection and combination of financial instruments. It is the purpose of this book to educate you in asset allocation so you will be able to make informed decisions for your own asset allocation. Whether you are new to investing or have been investing for some time, understand how different investments can work together to improve your portfolio and why you should choose one financial security over another.

Asset allocation is a simple and powerful concept and, when implemented correctly, will reduce risk, smooth out the fluctuations in returns, and provide profit whenever any section of the market experiences large gains. It will never realize the maximum gains that, in retrospect, could have been achieved by investing in a particular sector or stock that happened to soar. Few investors can consistently predict which those are going to be, so pursuing such a course is a high-risk strategy.

The key to asset allocation is finding investments that do not move together at the same time. The relationship between them is called the correlation. The correlation is perfect if the investments move in lock step, there is no correlation if the investments move totally independently of each other, and there is a negative correlation if one goes up when the other goes down.

When you are selecting assets to hold in your portfolio, consider your time horizon. This is the amount of time you will be investing or holding your portfolio before you expect to use it to achieve a financial goal, such as retirement. If it will be a long time before you need the funds, you can choose to take on a riskier portfolio that has the chance of producing higher returns. Such a portfolio can swing in value, but you can wait out the slower economic cycles because you do not need to access the money. If you are saving for an event a few years away, such as sending a teenager to college, your time horizon is shorter. If your portfolio suffers from dips in the market, you might find you have less money when you need it. If this is the case, you might have to settle for lower returns to invest in a less risky manner.

As we grow older, our financial needs change and our understanding of investments matures. If you are starting your portfolio when you are still years away from needing the money, you can afford the luxury of making some mistakes while exploring different investment strategies. Your portfolio generally will not be as large as that of an older person, so you do not have as much to lose. Also, you have more working years to make up the losses. It is much easier to recover from losing $5,000 on a $20,000 account at the age of 25 than it is from losing $50,000 on a $200,000 account when you are 50.

In addition, when you get older and your career is established, you can form a clearer picture of what your retirement should look like. This allows you to fund any savings and investment plans you have with the realism to achieve your goals. In their 50s and 60s, most people are at their peak earning years, and children will most likely have finished college and become self-sufficient. This should allow you to make more accurate predictions of how well your existing savings portfolio will translate into the type of retirement you are looking forward to and allow you to project a retirement date if you hope to retire early.

Many portfolios become more aggressive when people enter their senior years. If saving and asset allocation have been successful, you might have more money than you need for the remainder of your life. You can invest some of it in riskier securities with a higher return with the intention of creating more wealth to pass on to the heirs. Asset allocation should be a focus of your portfolio management throughout life but must change to reflect the circumstances as time passes. Your time horizon will vary, and your portfolio must reflect this.

Allocation versus Diversification

There is some confusion over the differences between asset allocation and asset diversification. Although some similarity and interaction are inevitable, they are two different ideas.

Asset diversification involves the distribution of assets over several different investments to reduce the potential for financial risk. Instead of making one huge investment in a market, the investor makes a number of small investments in different markets. The portfolio can be diversified at two levels. The first is between the different asset categories or market sectors, and the second is within each category or sector so the portfolio is not dependent on any one financial security.

Sometimes, diversification within a category is most easily achieved by owning a fund rather than individual equities because the number of different financial instruments can easily mount up and become hard to manage. The fund can be a mutual fund specializing in a particular market sector or a stock market index fund that allows you to own shares in all of the companies traded in that market. These can be effective techniques, but still examine them to achieve the goal of diversification. For instance, the mutual fund in a particular sector might invest heavily in just three or four companies if those are the ones the mutual fund manager believes will perform best. Also figure into the performance the fund's charges.

Asset allocation involves a mathematical formula that weighs the assumption of risk for certain asset classes. This process allows the investor to make informed decisions about how much risk he or she is willing to take in return for potential profits. Asset allocation can include real estate investments, equities, and other markets. *Chapter 5 looks at alternative investments, such as real estate, you might consider for your portfolio*. The perfect proportion of the different types of investment depends on the individual investor, the risk tolerance, current market volatility, and the various correlations between the assets in the portfolio.

Several factors affect the decisions investors make when they are putting together their asset allocation strategy. These factors, in broad terms, are the investor profile, investment outlook, and investment universe. Each plays a part in determining both the investor's behavior and the collective behavior of the markets.

The investor profile includes the length of time the portfolio will grow before it is needed. This, together with the outlook of the investor, affects the volatility he or she can accept both in the individual categories and for the portfolio as a whole.

The investment outlook shows how much patience and determination the investor will be able to maintain during those times when the portfolio performs over or under. Inevitably, investments do not progress uniformly, and the expectations are not always met. The outlook also includes the investor's confidence level in the forecasts of future performance, including the specific return, risk, and correlation forecasts the portfolio is based on.

The investment universe relates protection of principal to protection of purchasing power while recognizing risk to principal is an inherent part of increasing returns. It defines the role and the amount of core and noncore asset classes the portfolio must contain. Core asset classes are those that have a low correlation to one another and do not move in a related way, and the noncore asset classes are those that fall outside this classification.

Investment Evolution

During the last part of the 20th century, investors' behavior began evolving. This evolution had a significant effect on the way individual investors designed their investments. Starting in the 1950s and continuing into the 1980s, many individual investors were becoming educated in the concept of asset allocation. As a result, they were starting to use a variety of different investment strategies, which included investing in large-, mid-, and small-capitalization equities; value and growth stocks; and international and global equities.

Although they chose to invest in both established and new markets, many investors also included bonds in their portfolios at least for diversification. The turnover in investments during this period was low because most investors tended to hold on to their investments rather than buy and sell as the market changed. The turnover was also low because individual investors often obtained their equity exposure and other assets by investing in mutual funds rather than buying them on the direct market, and this meant the mutual fund manager took care of any minor adjustments in share holdings the market suggested.

During the 1980s and 1990s, changes in the financial markets caused many investors to shift their focus to domestic equity investments and away from fixed income securities, international equities, and value-based approaches to investing. During that same time, the number of investors who sought to take advantage of alternative equity asset classes, such as private equity, venture capital, real estate, and hedge funds, continued increasing. Investment turnover began increasing with the advent of new strategies formulated to allow the investors to create portfolios with absolute returns rather than relative returns. These placed more emphasis on the construction and selection of market benchmarks. Companies and individual investors were focusing on owning equities directly in addition to acquiring them through investments in mutual funds.

By the latter part of the 1990s, the volatility of the market caused some investors to lose faith in the value of asset allocation. Some investors were even questioning the validity of asset diversification, risk control, and long-term investment practices and preferred to select high-performing annual capital growth investments. Between 1995 and 2000, a huge influx of new technology companies took advantage of the growing popularity of the Internet, which earned this time period the title of the dot-com era. During this time, thousands of online companies made their appearance.

In addition to new online companies, more traditional companies began establishing an online presence. Companies were now expected to have a website. Between 1999 and 2000, the Federal Reserve increased interest rates a total of six times. In retrospect, this caused the economy to begin sagging and had a detrimental effect on many online companies. When the dot-com bubble burst, the abrupt drop in the NASDAQ composite index in early 2000 sent a shiver through the financial markets that affected many Internet, telecommunications, and technology stocks and caused a reversal of the earlier trends. This forced many investors to once again embrace the idea and practicality of asset allocation, or at least diversification, rather than believing it was unnecessary. The positive returns on well-managed hedge funds and on U.S. Treasury bonds showed a well-allocated portfolio would not have suffered such a serious crash.

Alternative investments, including absolute return strategies and a host of other techniques that involve derivative instruments, will be discussed in Chapter 5.

Investors should consider several factors when weighing strategies for asset allocation. When investing, look at the long term rather than just at today's market in which things could change as quickly as the end of the day or even in the next five minutes. The potential for such a short turnaround is one of the best arguments for both asset allocation and asset diversification. The following is a general guideline investors can use when choosing the best strategy for asset allocation and the components that comprise those asset allocation factors.

Income Statement Factors

Of the factors that might have a substantial bearing on an investor's choice of an asset allocation strategy, the income statement factors most directly influence the amount of profit investors can show. There might be losses in some investments, and the amount of loss an investor is able to tolerate during any investment period is influenced by several things, including one or more of the following:

- The severity of the loss expressed either as a percentage or in terms of the actual monetary loss
- The time period during which the loss is expected to affect the investor's portfolio
- Whether the loss has happened or is simply anticipated
- How the loss might affect the future price action
- The impact of the loss related to other investment instruments
- The general economic conditions at the time of the loss
- The emotional, financial, and psychological well-being of the individual investor

The feelings of other investors about the future of the market might have a substantial amount of influence on the strategic and tactical asset allocation strategies an individual investor will use. Part of this outlook would include the investor's strategic and tactical approaches given the length of time it will take him or her to reach targets for price and the precise nature of the price movements, which includes whether they are slow and steady or tend to spiral upward or downward sharply.

One of the most important differences between successful investors and the less successful are the flexibility and certainty each one possesses. These can be summed up as the individual investor's level of confidence. The investor who is certain of his or her projections will stand by those beliefs and refuse to bend even to the point of being proved wrong. Those who are able to accept the possibility of flaws in their judgments must have the flexibility to see their mistakes and be willing to change their projections whenever necessary. Failure to accept flaws in judgment and change decisions accordingly will result in the investors having less success than they would otherwise.

The investor's tax status, which includes other assets, has a huge bearing on the way he or she must structure asset allocation. This has to take into account all taxes, including federal, state, local, and any others that might be related to the particular portfolio. The taxes can include capital gains, estate taxes, and current and future tax liabilities based on the investor's income tax bracket and its potential to change.

Balance Sheet Factors

Items that are reflected on the balance sheet could also influence the decisions an investor would make about asset allocation. Although this is not necessarily information that will reflect profit or loss, it shows the value of the investor's assets.

Individual investors need to consider the goals and purpose of the assets that are part of an individual allocation. Each investor should keep an open mind and focus on the right reasons and motivations for his or her individual choices without being sidetracked by the needs of investors in general. Investors should consider who they are investing for, whether for themselves or for a dependent, and what those assets might mean to the individual circumstances of that beneficiary. The investor should also allow for any unforeseen circumstances that might arise.

Investors should consider any anticipated investment positions, capital flows, options, and securities that might have a restricted nature. At the same time, they have to consider all the investments as a whole to make the right choices. They should look at the merits and cost factors that would be involved if they were to assume a concentrated investment position instead of diversifying all or part of these investments into other asset classes.

Another factor is the amount of income the investor will need, forseen expenses, and the required margin for contingencies. The investor's level of financial need will heavily influence decisions about asset allocation. It might be necessary for an investor to choose asset classes and investments with fixed income rather than speculative results and to choose dependable cash flows to be able to meet financial obligations.

Many investors have a significant portion of their wealth rooted in items that are not normally considered part of a conventional investment plan. Some of this might include royalties from published works; interest in oil, gas, or other industries; collections of art, antiques, and other assets; ownership in personal real estate that is not investable real estate; or family businesses. Some of these can be included in the asset allocation, and all of these add to the general wealth of an investor as it relates to the balance sheet. But only some of them can be considered tradable and therefore part of the investment portfolio.

Factors Off the Balance Sheet

In addition to income statement and balance sheet factors, several other factors might also have a bearing on the way an investor chooses to structure asset allocation. Although these are not directly monetary in nature, they are important enough to consider when you are formulating your asset allocation strategy.

The first of the factors is timing, or when the investor or other beneficiary of the portfolio will require the invested capital in a certain form. This information is essential if you are to create a meaningful and effective asset allocation strategy that will give the desired results.

Another factor is in establishing goals and benchmarks relative to the anticipated returns. Setting goals for projected returns is an essential part of following investment activity. It is also an important part of helping the investor define and create the best asset allocation scheme to achieve those goals. Typical goals an investor might set include assuring the safety of the principal in the investment portfolio, preserving and protecting the purchasing power of the money invested, and specifying and protecting specific levels before and after tax returns.

An investor should be able to recognize and evaluate possible trade-offs. Looking at the entire portfolio and relating it to the financial market, the investor must be able to judge the cost factor as it relates to alternative assets. It might be necessary to weigh one factor against another to come up with the profile with the best cost-benefit ratio. Assess the relative merits of the benefits of one type of investment to see how it compares to another with a higher return or more substantial benefit.

CASE STUDY: ASSET ALLOCATION: IMPERATIVE TO INVESTOR SUCCESS

John Nowicki, president and CCO
LCM Capital Management
230 W. Monroe St., Suite 310
Chicago, IL, 60606
Phone: 312-705-3013
Fax: 312-705-5044
www.lcmcapital.com

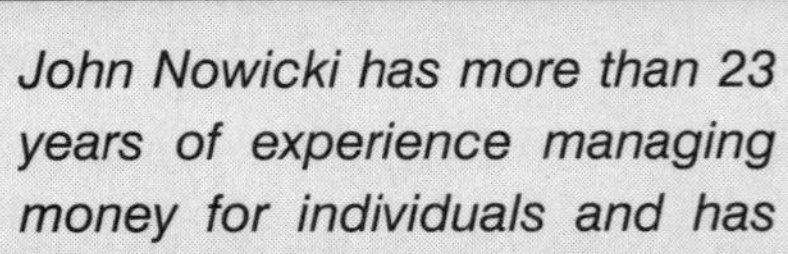

LCM Capital Management, Inc.

John Nowicki has more than 23 years of experience managing money for individuals and has spent the last 10 years as owner of LCM Capital Management Inc., a federally registered investment advisory firm based out of Chicago, Illinois. He presently holds the position of president and CCO.

If the last 10 years have shown investors anything, it is that asset allocation is not just important, it is imperative. Asset allocation removes the two greatest obstacles for investors: fear and greed. Once these emotions are removed, investor success increases dramatically.

The major benefits derived from using an asset allocation strategy include:

- Removing emotions of fear and greed from investment
- Lessening portfolio volatility and risk
- Lessening time wasted choosing investments and stocks and guessing when it is time to buy and sell
- Lessening time spent watching CNBC and Mad Money
- Increasing peace of mind

Asset allocation and diversification are different because asset allocation is a general overview of a portfolio, for example, how much one allocates to stocks, bonds, real estate, and cash. Diversification is the subcategories of stocks, for example large-cap, international and emerging markets, mid- and small-cap, and the maturities, underlying strength, and credit rating of bonds.

Asset allocation allows you to gauge risk at a macro level while diversification seeks to manage risk at the micro level.

Asset allocation does not work:

- Over the short term
- When investing into speculative areas, such as futures, options, and commodities
- When using leverage

When using an asset allocation strategy, the investor must consider he or she will be removing the thrill from investing and the emotions that come along with it, which is not a bad thing. They must also consider and realize the amount of discipline it will take to keep to the strategy and shut out external noises, influence, and friend's advice to make changes. In short, they must ignore the day-to-day fluctuations to benefit from the long-term results.

The risk profile of the investors we work with always matches their asset allocation strategy. All clients complete our risk questionnaire, a key component of determining their risk tolerance. Portfolios are established accordingly and managed to our asset allocation models. As a fiduciary, we have a contract with and an obligation to our clients to tell them how their assets will be allocated and determine through periodic contact whether changes in their lives, such as loss of job, income, or benefits, might require them to become more risk averse.

Portfolio rebalancing works to restore a portfolio to its intended asset allocation mix but not without discipline. By rebalancing, you will consistently sell high and buy low, which is what all investors strive for but few accomplish. If your holdings are 60 percent stock and 40 percent bonds and the bond market rallies, it comes at the expense of stocks, and the portfolio might shift to 50 percent stocks and 50 percent bonds. To rebalance to the intended risk of 60 percent stock and 40 percent bonds, you have to sell what was working, in this example bonds, and buy what was not working, in this example stocks. The problem is most investors want to keep buying what is working and sell what is not working.

In using asset allocation strategies with our clients, we keep things simple. All our clients own individual large-cap stocks, international stocks, and mid- and small-cap indices. This eliminates style drift, which I believe is a major reason for underperformance by investors and mutual funds. We ladder all fixed income with individual bonds across the maturity spectrum, which eliminates any guesswork on when interest rates will be moving higher or lower.

I believe asset allocation can hurt an investor's portfolio in the short term. If you are allocating your assets toward a highly speculative area or by using leverage, it could hurt the portfolio severely. If you keep your allocation simple, you will avoid major losses and also major gains. However, I have yet to come across any investors after more than 23 years who would not trade the larger upside for smaller downside once you explain and show them what happens. We firmly believe those who lose the least win the race and express this to all our clients.

I would not call the efficient frontier an accurate indicator of investor expectations relative to risk versus returns. I would hesitate to use the word accurate. A beginning guideline might be more appropriate. As most investors have found out over the past 10 years, risk is difficult to measure because of the complexity of most investment products firms have created and investors are willing to buy. Additionally, the lack of transparency within the industry can mask or hide the total risk.

Individual Investors versus Professional Investors

How do you differentiate between an individual investor and a professional investor? In which way do they think differently when it comes to investing and asset allocation? The principal distinguishing feature is individual investors are like you. They do not belong to an investment firm or other professional organization, and this has a significant impact on the approach they take to financial matters. These differences are also apparent in other aspects of life; the psychology and the way people behave have a substantial effect on the way they plan for asset allocation. These characteristics can have a positive or negative influence on the way an investor structures his or her asset allocation or fails to do so.

Some individuals believe professional and institutional investors have an advantage because they have better access to tools, such as research, corporate management, other means of communication, and access to other investors on the same level. If they allow these feelings of inferiority to become part of the investment strategy, they might be ill-equipped to make the decisions necessary to create a highly successful and profitable portfolio.

An individual investor might have an advantage over the corporate or professional investor. As a business owner or an employee of the company, such an individual might possess a vast knowledge of the business world. This potentially places him or her in a better position than the corporate or professional investor to assess the effect crop cycles, energy costs, inflation, and other events might have on movement in the price of investments. This knowledge is essential and pertinent for an investor to develop correct asset allocation strategy and be assured of a higher income ratio and return on investment. This is not to say professional investors do not have access to this information, but their focus is more on the trends as they relate to the corporate and institutional investor rather than the individual investor.

Another advantage individual investors have over professional investors is they have no one else to answer to but themselves.

There is no board of directors or group of stockholders waiting for an answer to the results of the latest investment. They need no one's approval to withdraw their funds from a specific asset class or security, a move that could make a more efficient and profitable portfolio.

Individual investors are capable of clear thinking, objectivity, and perception. They might not always exert these qualities and sometimes tend to believe they are not as independently capable as they are. However, because his or her funds are involved in the investment, the individual investor is less capable of withstanding a substantial loss. For some individual investors, this fact clarifies their way of thinking and allows them to make better judgments about asset allocation and diversification. For others, this clouds their vision and prevents them from making financially feasible decisions about the investments.

Individual investors have as great an ability to make sound judgments as institutions and professional investors do. Sound judgment might often be lacking in the investment world even though every investor and potential investor is capable of using it to ensure high returns. Sound judgment allows the investor to make the right choices when it involves asset classes and in asset allocation strategies. The combination of sound judgment and proper asset allocation use will increase individual or professional investors' opportunities and help increase their profits.

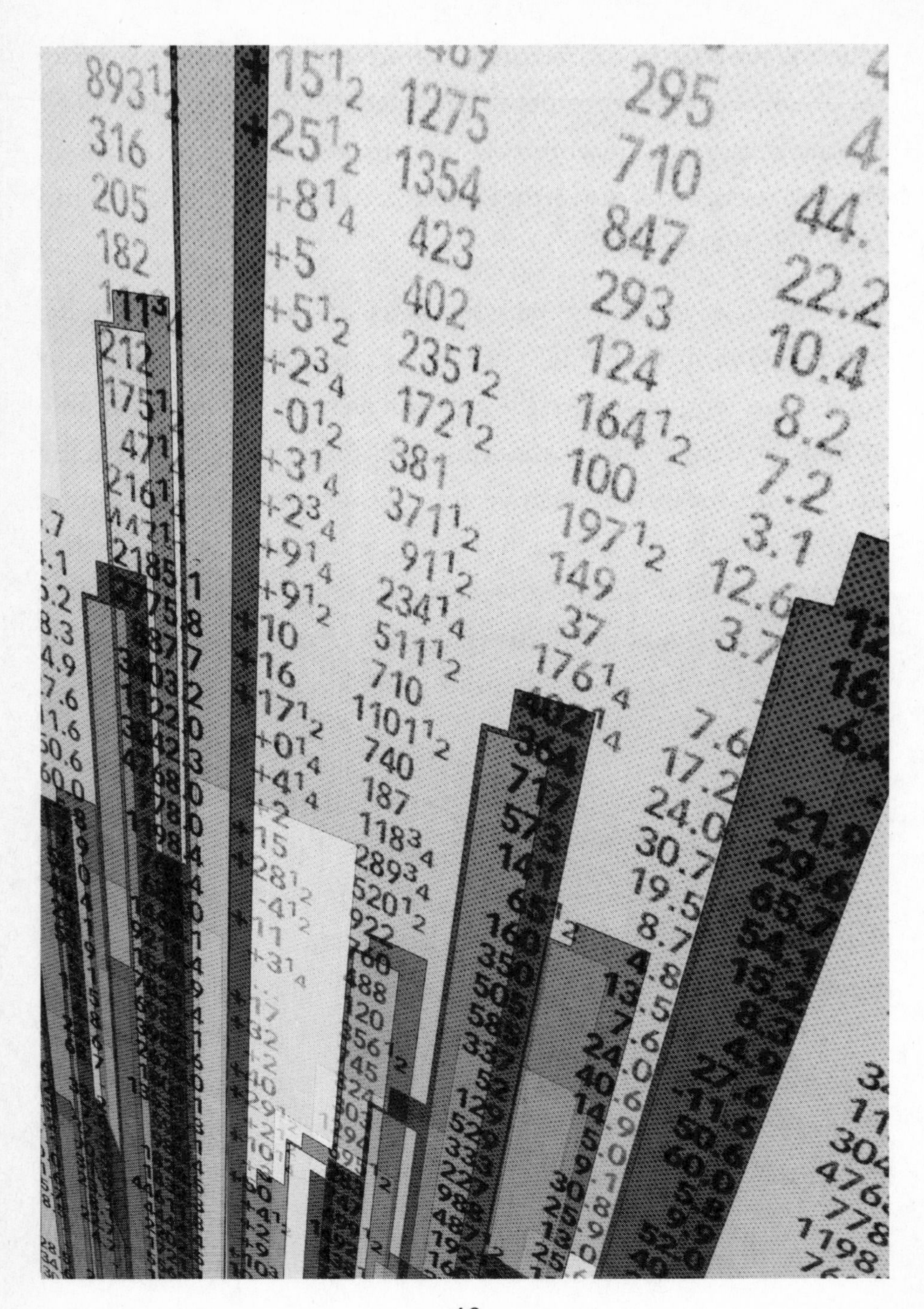

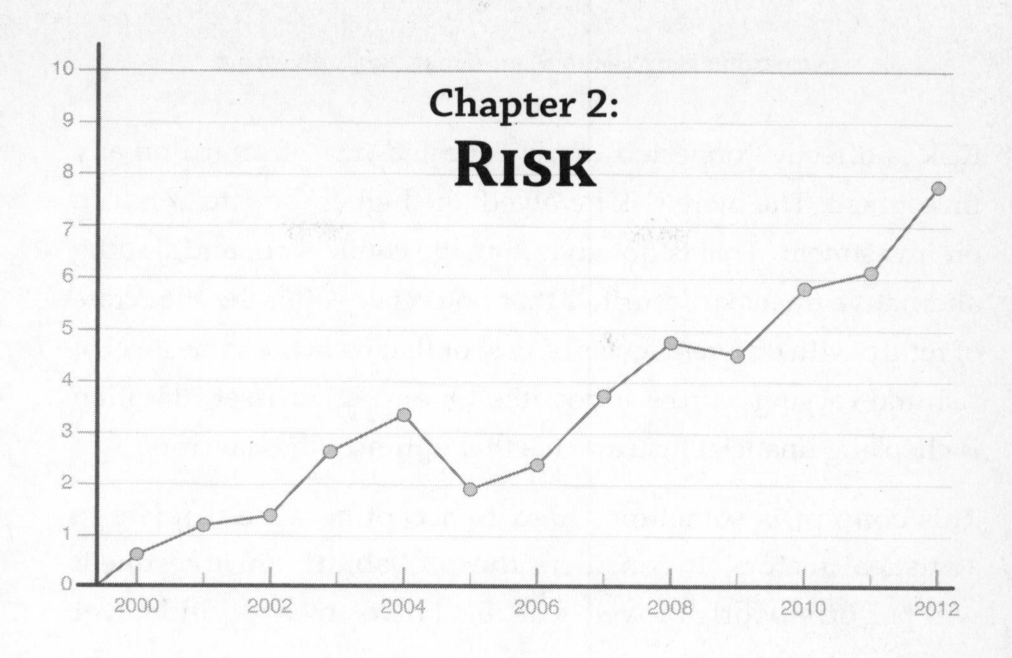

Chapter 2: Risk

BEFORE YOU LOOK AT THE DIFFERENT ASSET CLASSES YOU could consider for your portfolio, it is necessary to understand risk and its ramifications. Risk can mean different things to different people and might change meaning in different circumstances, so you need to review the various concepts related to risk.

Only you can decide your tolerance for risk, which will determine your correct asset allocation. Risk has many facets, but in general terms, it is the chance that you might lose some or all of your original investment in exchange for potentially greater returns. If you are an aggressive investor, you will take on more risk in an endeavor to get better results. A conservative investor will try to preserve the original investment even if the profits are not so great. This will be discussed in more detail later.

Risk is directly connected to the expected rate of return on any investment. The more risk involved, the higher the rate of return on investment. This is not an automatic connection, and finding alternative financial securities that potentially offer the same rate of return with different levels of risk, or that have the same level of risk and varying returns, is possible. One aspect of asset allocation is choosing financial instruments that optimize these factors.

This concept is sometimes hard to accept because it refers to statistical factors. It considers the probability an investment will perform poorly or well. The ideal investment would never perform poorly or at least would be guaranteed to achieve the desired result at the end of the time horizon when the money is required. There is no such thing as a guarantee in the investment business, so you must settle for the best experts can determine from statistics and the likelihood of the performance you want. Even a low-risk investment has a chance of falling in value, and you might be lucky with a high-risk investment and never lose any money. All you can do is stack the odds in your favor and be comforted by full knowledge of what the outcome is expected to be.

The overriding notion is you cannot expect to get a return for no investment. If you want to earn a high rate of return, you must face the fact there will be some risk involved. Risk can come in many forms. The risk you could lose 25 percent of your account once every 10 years might equate mathematically to losing 5 percent of your account five times in 10 years, but you would probably regard these risks differently.

Every asset or investment has its own unique risk and return characteristics. When you combine them into a portfolio, it has unique risk and return characteristics which are unlike any of the constituents. *Chapter 7 will look at how all these hypothetical factors can be analyzed and results can be generated.* However, no matter how much detail or accuracy is applied to the calculation, it is only an estimation of what the odds favor happening, not a prediction of what will happen. These specifics can be left until later.

When you design a portfolio, you should do so to achieve a higher risk-adjusted return from it than from each of the individual investments used. This is the essence of asset allocation and the reason it is considered so worthwhile. Combining assets that are complementary in this way can achieve a portfolio that is greater than the sum of its parts.

CASE STUDY: THE BENEFITS OF ASSET ALLOCATION

Versie Walker
PO Box 1111
Hopewell Jct., NY, 12533
Phone: (877) 412-6398
Fax: (888) 390-0232.
info@newlookpublishing.com
www.versiewalker.com

Versie L. Walker is a Hudson Valley author, entrepreneur, and public speaker. Originally from Chicago, Walker has more than 20 years of experience in sales. Self-taught, he earned several professional licenses, including being a Series 7 financial advisor. During his corporate career, he worked for JP Morgan Chase, Bank of New York, and Prudential Life. He is the author of Success, How I Ended Up Here!, *published by New Look Publishing (**http://newlookpublishing.com**).*

Asset allocation helps an individual investor see that spreading risk among various asset classes could conceivably reduce the amount of risk to the principal invested and still achieve a high rate of return.

Several benefits are derived from using an asset allocation strategy. It adds diversity to a well-rounded investment portfolio that should always include individually held securities, such as stocks, bonds, and mutual funds. More importantly, it helps an investor lower his or her risk during the investment period. Some like to think of it as being able to sleep at night. The returns are not as high as investing in one or more individually traded securities, but neither are the risks.

A good allocation model will automatically reset the investor's portfolio percentage across the various asset classes, which helps maintain the original asset allocation model for the client, for example, 25 percent placed in tech, 25 percent placed in biochem, and 50 percent placed in blue chip stock. Your advisor or the allocation model will reset to the original percentage. This can be done either daily, weekly, or quarterly to prevent overweighting in any asset class. Simple diversification would not do this.

There are always cases in which asset allocation does not work. For example, your percentage weighting was too high or not high enough during a given period, and your portfolio performed less than the market or less than what you expected. There are no guarantees when it comes to investing. However, a good asset allocation model can help minimize a lot of the guesswork and frustration, and you can change it whenever you like.

Whenever investing, always consider these things:

- **Time horizon:** How long will it be before you will need these funds?
- **Risk tolerance:** How much risk are you willing to take with your principal investment?
- **Time value of money:** How much will your investment be worth in the future, or what will today's invested dollars be worth in the future with the current rates of return and inflation?

Based on the questionnaire all investment advisors must provide each customer, the risk profile of the investors should match their asset allocation strategy. However, there are many cases in which a client might have believed they were one type of investor, and the answers provided in their risk profile questionnaire show differently. It then becomes the job of the investment advisor to go over the information with the client and get clear directions for how the client wishes to proceed.

Portfolio rebalancing does work to restore the portfolio to its intended asset allocation mix. The process of rebalancing is something many fund and portfolio managers now offer as part of their advisory services. This process can be done as frequently as daily, weekly, or quarterly, and you and your advisor can decide how often this should be done in your particular case. The process is to maintain the integrity of the initial allocation mix, for example, 20 percent in one sector, 40 percent in another, and 40 percent in yet another. Should one class or sector under or overperform and make up more or less of the portfolio's percentage in a class, the rebalance returns a portfolio back to its original allocation mix.

As a former financial advisor for various banks, including Bank of New York and J.P. Morgan Chase, I used asset allocation strategies with clients as a way to demonstrate how they could achieve the investment objectives while minimizing risk and reducing exposure to market fluctuation in any one asset class. This worked well with clients who were somewhat risk adverse but still wanted some market performance and exposure.

In some cases, asset allocation could hurt an investor's portfolio returns. However, if done properly, it could hedge against steep declines if the market turned and could provide better returns than those of bank-backed products during market highs. If the client is looking for better performance and is not concerned with return of principal, he or she might not need this aspect of asset allocation and should perhaps buy the individual securities represented in most allocation models.

When I was first introduced to the efficient frontier more than eight years ago, it was said to be an accurate indicator of investor expectations relative to risk versus returns, and from what I was able to tell, it was. However, as we all know, times have changed, and since the events of the past two and a half years, individuals' tolerance to risk versus returns has drastically changed. Investors are now more inclined to lean toward safer investments, if they invest at all, and are more concerned with the return of their money than they are with the return on their money.

Risk-free Investing

If you are prepared to accept a low return, you might think you can find a risk-free investment, such as a U.S. Treasury bill, which is government guaranteed. Given that you do not expect the U.S. government to renege on its promises and that the government can always print new money, the return on a U.S. Treasury bill seems as certain as death and taxes.

Although you can be fairly confident of a return on your investment, it is not necessarily true to call it risk-free. The return you get from a Treasury bill is subject to erosion of its value from inflation and taxes. Here is a chart showing how inflation has resulted in a negative return for a significant portion of the past ten years:

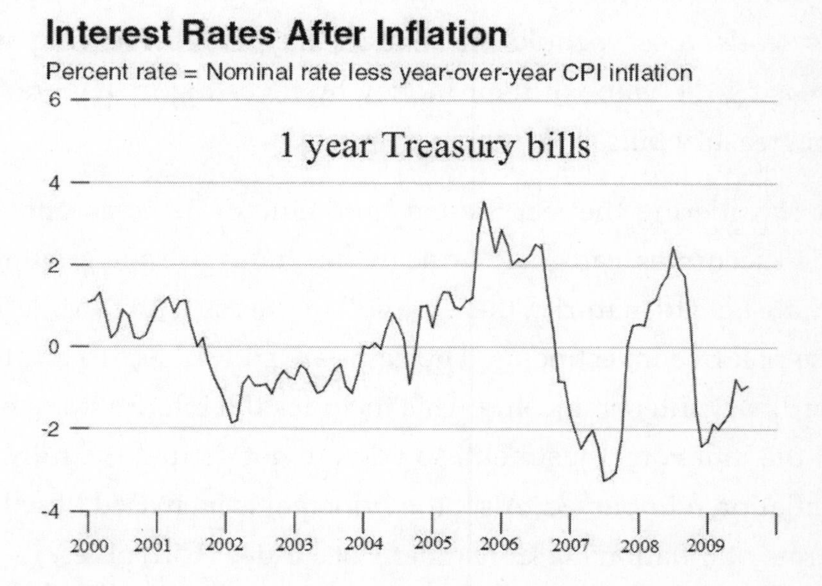

The chart was compiled from figures released by the Federal Reserve Bank. It only takes into account the impact of inflation, but depending on your tax situation, your returns might be even lower. If short-term interest rates are lower than the inflation rate, investing in Treasury bills — and in money market funds that have a similar rate of return — is costing you spending power. If you take the rate of return that has been offered for the last 50 years, continually reinvesting your money in Treasury bills, you will find you have less than you started with after tax and inflation. This does not seem to qualify as a risk-free investment by any reasonable definition.

A relatively new type of investment is the Treasury Inflation Protected Security (TIPS). The maturity value of this bond increases in direct proportion to the amount of inflation. Even the interest paid during the holding period increases with inflation. This leads most people to believe they are preserving and increasing the value of their money by investing in TIPS rather than Treasury bills.

Not considering the fact the current value of TIPS, as publicly traded securities, can go down as interest rates rise and assuming they are held to maturity, there are still problems with considering these risk-free investments. The gains are still subject to taxation as ordinary interest income. This includes the interest payments and the inflation adjustment, so you are not getting the full cost of inflation reimbursed. Also, the principal is increased based on the rate of inflation the Consumer Price Index (CPI) gives.

There has been much criticism of the CPI and whether it reflects the cost of living. Increases in government payments, such as social security, are also tied into this index, and there are a number of accusations that the way the CPI is calculated has been changed over the years with a bias toward making inflation appear less than what the majority of consumers experience. Thus, even to keep up with the CPI is not necessarily to keep up with the increases in the cost of living most people experience. You can find more details on the criticism of CPI on the Internet.

How Much Risk?

The easiest way to define risk in the financial markets is to say it is a fluctuation in the value of an investor's portfolio. How much risk is felt depends how often the investor is used to checking the portfolio. For instance, if the investor checks the value of the portfolio several times in a month, he or she will view the investment risk in the light of these short-term fluctuations. In this case, regular weekly fluctuations of a few percentage points might prove too much for the investor to tolerate.

Under other circumstances, such fluctuations might not matter. If the investor is solely concerned about the long term — and comfortable with the statistical variations of a particular portfolio — the chief risk might be the potential for the portfolio to not increase in value enough to achieve the target amount several years in the future. So risk must be seen in the context of what matters to the investor and what might keep him or her awake at night.

Another term you hear when talking about the risk of investment is volatility. Sometimes the words risk and volatility are even used interchangeably. They are not the same but are closely related.

Volatility is clearly defined and can be statistically measured as how varied the returns are for a particular security or financial instrument. This measurement can be the statistical deviation or taken from the variance between returns. The higher the volatility, the more the value can vary from the average and the more risky the investment. An academic might be inclined to consider risk as the volatility of returns on investment measured over different periods of time. For example, large value swings from month to month could be equated to high volatility, which might also be regarded as high risk.

A factor to consider with volatility is it can affect the value of the portfolio over the long term, which would be measured as standard deviation. This is the variance between the current return on the fund and its previous performance or the average performance of similar funds. Funds that have a higher standard deviation have demonstrated a high potential to fluctuate from the fund's average performance. The standard deviation is calculated by subtracting the average return from the actual returns for an individual security. The differences or deviations are squared before being added together to obtain the variance. The square root of the variance is called the standard deviation.

The higher the standard deviation, the more the return on investment varies from the average. Thus, a portfolio paying an annual return of 8 percent with a standard deviation of 0 percent will earn a higher return than a portfolio paying an annual return of 9 percent with a standard deviation of 18 percent. When you are looking for a portfolio that will provide the highest return over the long term, look at the standard deviation and not just the average return.

If you are running a mutual fund, you might regard risk as the possibility your fund will not perform as well as other comparable funds. The fund manager who underperforms the sector tends to lose clients and ultimately might lose his or her job. Whether the swings in value are large or small is not so significant, so volatility is of secondary importance.

If you are more concerned with the long-term view, as the manager of a pension fund would be, your definition of risk is likely to concern whether the fund can meet future pension obligations. Unlike the mutual fund manager, whose clients might dissipate within a few months of bad fund performance compared to others, the pension fund manager is concerned not with client retention but meeting commitments that have been taken on over the years. The calculation involves estimating the return on assets into the future and balancing this against the assumed pension payments, which leads the manager to determine whether the pension fund was fully funded. An underfunded plan is a problem, and if the plan is run on behalf of an employer, it might mean the employer has to commit resources that were not budgeted to keep the plan solvent.

Individual's Risk

Taking the view of the individual investor, think of risk more as losing money. The psychology of losing money is somewhat akin to driving in heavy traffic with two parallel lanes that make irregular progress. When you are overtaking the adjacent lane, everything is fine. When the other lane is progressing faster than you, each car that passes creates more stress. It does not matter if, on average, both lanes are moving at the same speed because that is irrelevant to the way you feel about it. You feel the loss of position much more strongly than any gains.

The same applies to considering your investment account. Your account might follow the market and be up 35 percent in the middle of one year, as the S&P 500 was in 1987. However, the subsequent losses before the end of the year, which finally left the S&P 500 up only 5 percent, were much more memorable to most investors who regarded 1987 as the year of the crash. Investors who were in the market for the whole year finished up but did not feel as though they did.

Sometimes, you should take a larger view than is natural. No investor, despite his or her purpose or job function, wants to lose money, but this is what he or she must risk to achieve positive inflation-adjusted returns. Even with well-calculated asset allocation, each individual investment that makes up your portfolio will act on its own terms, and the coincidence of these events sometimes will result in your portfolio going down. All you can hope to do is mitigate the losses and reduce the occurrence by implementing asset allocation.

Of all the ways of looking at risk, the most practical is that of the pension fund manager. Unless you need money right away, in which case you should secure your funds in a money market or equivalent account, the real function of your portfolio is to provide the value you need at some time in the future. Running out of funds during retirement is a recurring nightmare for some people, and preserving and growing cash for the long term is a common goal.

Volatility Losses

One point to emphasize about high volatility investments and returns is it is not enough to rely on the simple average annual return of an investment when considering its value in your portfolio. The volatility of the investment will affect the actual return you receive. This is an extension of the idea that you require a greater percentage increase to make up a percentage loss.

As an example, assume your portfolio loses 25 percent. It is not enough for you to invest for a return of 25 percent to restore it. You need a return of 33 1/3 percent to get back to where you started. $100,000 reduces to $75,000 if you lose 25 percent. You need to gain 33 percent, or $25,000, to restore the account.

Similarly, if you lost half of your account, you would need gains of 100 percent to return to the original value. The simple average return for the first example would be (-25+33.333)/2, which is 4.17 percent. The simple average return for the second case is (-50+100)/2, which is 25 percent. If you had invested at a constant 3 percent return, you would be better off and would have increased the value of your original portfolio by more than 6 percent rather than simply having the same amount of money at the end.

Note how the simple mechanics of calculating percentages can be misleading. If you made 25 percent on your investment, you would only have to suffer a 20 percent loss to be back where you started. Making money seems to be an uphill task compared with the simplicity of losing it. A volatile investment, which has high gains and losses, will lose you much more money than you realize if you just look at the simple average percentages.

One of the most difficult concepts for many investors to understand is choosing between risk and return. New investors seem to feel they should be able to create a perfect portfolio that will provide large returns with little or no risk. This perfect portfolio does not exist, but investors have other options to ensure they are not burdened with an enormous loss in the event that one of their investments turns out to be less than profitable. Risk is something that comes with any portfolio no matter how careful the investor might be. The key is to learn how to create a portfolio that provides the highest returns with the least amount of risk.

The key to maximizing profits and reducing risk is through the Modern Portfolio Theory (MPT), a topic the book discusses in more depth in later chapters. In brief, this involves diversification although simple diversification in itself is not sufficient to optimize your portfolio. There are no guarantees on the amount of return any investment will provide, but by exercising due diligence, the investor can ensure his or her portfolio produces stable returns at least in the long run. The investor should also learn how to effectively exercise diversification and asset allocation. The combination of these two elements within the investor's portfolio is the best way to ensure the lowest risk and the highest return on investment.

Although no investments are without some measure of risk, the investor can train in those aspects that allow him or her to choose investments with the least amount of risk. For the short-term investor, the risks will be higher because there is less time to recover from any losses. In addition, the short-term investor is looking for higher returns during a shorter period of time than the long-term investor, who might be looking for a high return on investment but has a better opportunity to recover any losses that occur along the way.

The long-term investor looks toward the future and knows returns might be lower in the beginning but will be compensated with higher returns later. Although this might be difficult for a new investor to understand, he or she should maintain some level of optimism for long-term investment and not worry over short-term losses no matter how substantial they seem. There has not been a 10-year period since 1950 during which stocks have not shown positive returns. The same cannot be said for Treasury bills and bonds. This shows the importance of considering investments for the long term rather than the short term.

Another important factor is standard deviation. Any investor must consider the effect of standard deviation when he or she chooses the asset classes and asset allocation strategy. Part of your asset allocation strategy should focus on choosing the assets that have the lowest standard deviation even though they might have a lower rate of return in the short term. Look at all possible scenarios to ensure you maximize your returns.

Risk and return have a general relationship in the financial markets. A temporary loss, although unpleasant, can be tolerated if it is part of an asset allocation strategy that will lead to high returns. Careful allocation and combination of different asset classes in a portfolio would manage risk and increase the chance of financial success.

Finally, to maximize your returns, accept the facts. No portfolio comes without some measure of risk, and the higher the return, the more risk the investor must assume. This simple fact has a substantial bearing on both asset diversification and asset allocation strategies. The investor must plan his or her strategy based on the amount of risk he or she is willing or able to tolerate for a long-term or a short-term investment. The investor must also keep in mind the volatility of the market, which will have a definite effect on the standard deviation and risk curve for that asset class.

This book will help the new investor learn everything necessary about asset allocation, including the MPT and the importance of asset allocation. You will also learn how to choose asset classes and use asset allocation to build an efficient and profitable portfolio. By the end of the book, you should feel confident about choosing asset classes and building an asset allocation strategy.

12 DIGIT 2 COLOR PRINTER
COST
SELL
MGN
AVG
GT
TAX+
TAX−

Chapter 3: Stocks

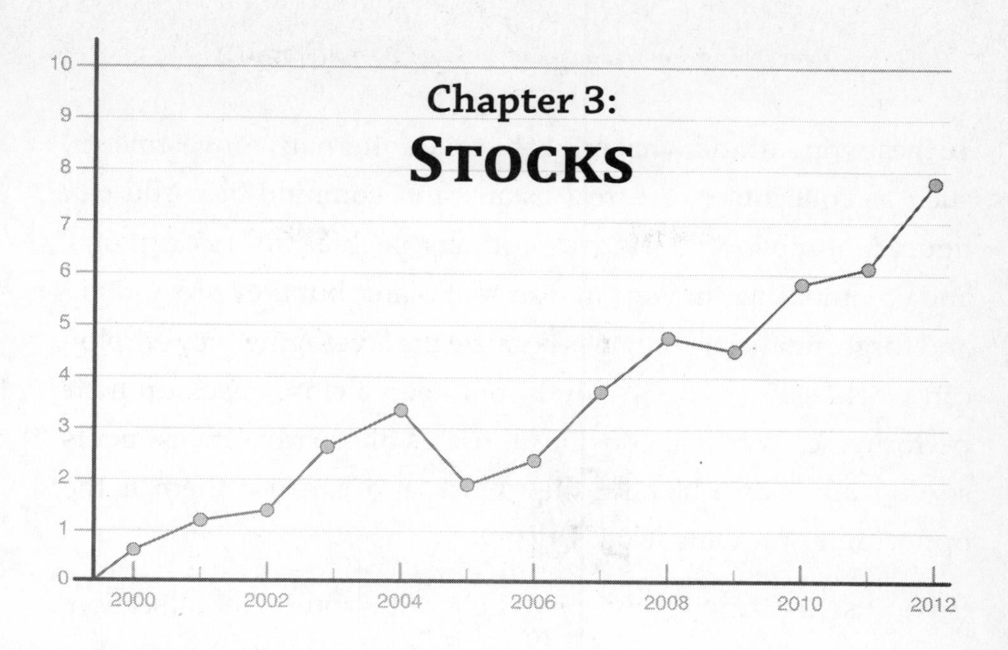

CHAPTER 1 SET THE STAGE FOR ASSET ALLOCATION AND *explained its value*. Now is the time to look in more detail at the selection of asset classes that are available and their characteristics so you are familiar with them when it becomes time to discuss the allocation.

Assets are traditionally broken down into three classes:

- Stocks, or equities
- Bonds, or fixed income investments
- Cash, or cash equivalents

These are the main categories, but they can be invested in various ways. For instance, using mutual funds to invest in many different types of financial instruments is common. More recently, exchange traded funds have come to the fore, and a comparison of the advantages and disadvantages will come later.

To these you can add what might be called alternative investments, such as collectibles, art, real estate, and commodities. You can figure a number of leveraged products, such as futures, options, and commodities, in your investment plans, but they are not buy and forget financial securities because the leveraging they employ can work against you if you do not keep a close check on their performance. We will consider those as alternative investments so you are aware of how they work and can use them if the opportunity presents itself.

If you use a financial advisor to help with your asset allocation, he or she will likely concentrate on investing in stocks whether directly or through a fund, bond holdings, and cash or money market equivalents. But with the knowledge you gain from this book, you can incorporate other investments to help your portfolio.

Stocks, or equities, have the highest degree of risk of any of the ordinary asset classifications, but they also produce the highest returns on average. In the context of asset allocation, stocks are held for extended periods, and the longer stocks are held, the more likely they are to revert to the mean and give a good return. Stocks of large corporations tend to move in cycles and will go through a losing cycle every few years, but if you are investing for the long-term and can ride out the volatile periods, you will be rewarded statistically with substantial growth over time. An investment portfolio that will require a return in a few years will tend to have a lower proportion of stocks to avoid the possibility of getting caught out by the volatility.

Domestic Equities

Stocks are at the core of most investment portfolios. This is for good reason because over the years the real return from the stock market has proven to be better than the other investments. Although the returns can be high, this asset class carries the most risk and should comprise only a part of your investment. About 150,000,000 Americans currently own stocks, and this includes direct ownership through stock purchase and indirect ownership through mutual funds, retirement accounts, and other investment pools.

Even within the U.S. markets, a wealth of in stocks is available. Although economic difficulties can affect the whole stock market, as we have seen in recent years, it is possible to find stocks that have little or negative correlation with each other that would form a good basic combination for risk reduction in a portfolio. If you understand the structure of the equity market, you are better able to select a diversified portfolio.

Over the years, investing in U.S. equities has provided investors with profitable returns. In the 20th century, the United States prospered, and many new companies started while established companies grew larger and stronger. Even with the disruption of two world wars, the U.S. economy experienced substantial growth in earnings, and investors in the United States companies grew accustomed to reliable dividend payments and increasing stock values.

Between 1963 and 1993, the average market return on U.S. stocks was 11.83 percent annually according to figures the University of Michigan published, which is substantially more than the return on bonds or the rate of inflation. In the 1990s, the longest bull market in history, the average annual returns were 18 percent, according to Ibbotson Associates. Yet between 1966 and 1982, which was the last protracted bear market, the Dow fell from 995 to 777. Even during this period, there were some notable bull rallies of up to 76 percent.

The volatility of the stock market can easily be seen from these figures. It is difficult to make an accurate projection of real returns, and sometimes the returns are not much higher than the rate of inflation. If you invest in the stock market, you should expect to see some periods of time when the equities do not show a profit after inflation adjustment, and this is part of the risk investors take by putting their money in the stock market.

The IPO

A company sells stock to the public for the first time through a process called the initial public offering (IPO). Run by investment bankers who are specially commissioned to distribute and promote the sale of the shares, this procedure is tightly controlled. Rather than trying to convince thousands of small investors to buy shares, the investment bankers talk to their current business associates and contacts in financial institutions about the merits of the IPO. This way, they can place large blocks or numbers of shares with buyers, which makes the IPO run more smoothly. This is why it is often difficult for the small investor to buy shares in an IPO, particularly if the initial issue is expected to be popular.

After the IPO process has happened and the shares have been sold to the market, the shares then start trading on the regular stock market, and everyone has an opportunity to buy them. The company received the IPO money, which might go toward funding expansion or another purpose. Once the shares are on the open market, all trading takes place between different parties, and the company does not benefit from it.

How and on which stock market the shares are traded depends on various factors. Only half of all the U.S. stocks that are actively traded qualify to be listed on a major stock exchange. The decision is based on the financial history of the company and on the value. If the company is not qualified to have its shares listed on the New York Stock Exchange (NYSE), the American Stock Exchange (AMEX), or the NASDAQ, it will be a pink sheet company, and its shares will be called bulletin board stocks. These can be traded through a broker who has access to that market. Bulletin board stocks became known as pink sheets many years ago when the prices were published weekly on long sheets of pink paper for distribution to brokers.

When you own stocks, you own part of the company, so you are entitled to profit payments that are made through dividends. You might expect the share price to appreciate if the company is performing well. Dividends are often paid every quarter, and companies that pay dividends tend to continue to do so and increase the amount paid out each time. It is a good policy for them to continue regular payments because the market takes it as a bad sign if they miss or reduce the dividends, and the share value might decrease.

Not all companies pay dividends to their shareholders, and investors in these companies will be hoping for the share price to increase so they achieve capital gains on their investment. Of course, if the company performs badly with falling sales, the price of the shares will likely drop. This volatility is what makes some investors wary of investing in stocks. Should a company go bankrupt, the common shareholders would receive any funds from the winding up and selling off of the company after creditors and bondholders.

Analysis

There are two basic ways of evaluating stocks and shares. These are called technical analysis and fundamental analysis. Technical analysis is primarily used in trading and relatively short-term buying and selling of equities. It is designed to provide tools that gauge investor sentiment and indicate the expected imminent movement of share prices. Technical analysis is the study of current trends. It evaluates how price and volume action can give clues to market sympathies and allow profitable short-term trading.

The other side of stock analysis, which is called fundamental analysis, pays closer attention to basic or fundamental factors of the companies involved. It is used to determine the long-term viability of the company and direction of share prices. Although technical analysis indicates market sympathy, and therefore where the market thinks the price will go right now, fundamental analysis looks at the background that will move the price in the long term and where the market should move the price over time. For an investment portfolio, fundamental analysis must be the root of stock selection.

For investment purposes, understand fundamental analysis whether you use financial advisors to help in particular stock selection. Understand the various factors and their relevance in determining the underlying and long-term value of the shares you are considering, including in your portfolio. When looking at the company's balance sheets, consider a wealth of factors, including operating cash flow, revenue, gross margins, and earnings before interest, taxes, depreciation, and amortization (EBITDA). One simple way you can get a feel for the strength and valuation of the company without taking an accountancy course is by using valuation ratios, which make for easy comparisons.

Perhaps the best-known gauge of a company's strength is the price/earnings (P/E) ratio, which is probably the most widely reported and used valuation method. For the general market, this has historically been around 15 although it does fluctuate depending on economic and market conditions and might be different in different sectors and industries. In essence, the P/E ratio shows you how much you are paying for every one dollar of earnings. It is simple to calculate although there is some variation in how earnings are reported. In practice, you want to compare the company's P/E ratio with the market, with the industry sector, and with two or three companies who are direct competitors. This will give you a feel for whether the stock price is high, low, or in the middle before you invest.

Before going any further into valuation ratios, look at some concepts of how they are calculated. Most valuation ratios relate back to the share price, and they give you an important guide to whether the stock you are interested in is over or undervalued. The share price is unambiguous even if subject to daily fluctuations, but some of the other values to which it is compared can be calculated in different ways. Most per-share data can be found in the corporate reports, such as the annual report, and forms 10-K and 10-Q, which are filed with the SEC.

The number of shares that are outstanding in the market can be viewed in different ways because companies can issue stock options, convertible preferred shares, and other forms that would increase the number of companies' shares outstanding if they were taken up. This is called a dilution because an increasing number of shares dilute the earnings and other amounts when viewed on a per-share basis. Therefore, earnings per share can be considered in two ways. The first is on the basis of the number of shares in existence. The second is on the basis of the number of shares that could be taken up if all issued options were exercised, which is the diluted earnings per share. The common ratios are calculated with the number of shares in existence.

When sales, earnings growth, and cash flow are given as per-share ratios, the average number of shares outstanding is used. To calculate the book value per share, the number of shares outstanding at the financial year's end is the relevant figure, and this way to provide the reports is the industry standard.

A big difference between the basic earnings per share and the diluted earnings per share might represent a problem in the future and be a red flag for anyone considering investing in the company. If a number of the option holders decide to exercise their option, the number of shares in the market would increase dramatically and the company's share price could fall in relation. With those caveats, valuation ratios are useful for providing an investor with a simplistic guideline of whether a stock price is too high, too low, or just right. Make sure the valuation ratios are calculated in a similar manner when comparing companies.

P/E ratio

The P/E ratio is the most widely reported measure of a company's strength, and some investors seldom consider anything further than this. In simple terms, it is the stock price per share divided by the earnings per share, but which numbers are used is important. The stock price is easily obtained from the Internet or from your broker, but earnings are subject to interpretation.

The earnings per share can be based on historical figures and will cover the 12 months leading up to the last quarterly report. The actual number of shares outstanding rather than the diluted number is used for this. Often, trailing P/E is the term used to describe this ratio to distinguish it from other types. A P/E ratio is also reported by using a projection of future earnings, which is an estimated P/E. The earnings per share used are estimates of the future 12-month earnings research analysts prepare.

The independent stock research firm Value Line, which publishes the Value Line Investment Survey weekly, developed a variation on these two forms of P/E ratios. It combines both systems by including data from the previous six months with data estimated for the next six months for the earnings per share part of the calculation.

You might come across several other types of P/E ratios. Sometimes businesses will report the cash earned per share, rather than the net income, based on the operating cash flow. In certain circumstances, companies will report based on a particular operating aspect of the company called other earnings per share. Generally, these lesser-known systems should be viewed with suspicion and do not provide a good reference for comparison with others.

Whichever P/E ratio you choose to use, make sure you use the equivalent with other companies or sectors when making comparisons. Unless the ratios are calculated in a similar way, your assessment of the company in question might be flawed.

The analysis of the P/E ratio is simple in principle. If a stock has a high P/E ratio, the price is high in comparison with the earnings. The price is based on supply and demand from investors, so the high price means investors are prepared to pay more in anticipation of future growth in earnings. Therefore, these stocks are considered to be growth stocks. The growth investor would regard this as an attractive buy.

The opposite of this, a stock with a low P/E ratio, would instead attract value investors who would not be inclined to buy stocks that appear to be overpriced, such as growth stocks. The value investor will look for stocks that can be seen as undervalued, which the low P/E ratio would imply, and hope to buy them at a bargain price in anticipation of the value being realized later.

Depending on the aims of the investor, a stock can have a low or a high P/E ratio and still be attractive to someone. Despite the amount of attention the P/E ratio gets, it is not a clear indicator that you must buy a particular stock because the expectation of future direction is built into the ratio. Nonetheless, the investment community extensively uses it, and it is probably the first metric many investors look at. It is best used in comparisons to get a sense of where a stock is headed. You can compare the P/E ratio to historical levels for the same stock and also to P/E ratios of similar companies to get a good sense of how the shares are behaving and which price is fair.

Other ratios

The P/E ratio has been refined, and the result is the price/earnings to growth ratio, or PEG. This ratio looks at estimated growth to see how it relates to the P/E ratio. It tries to validate the growth investors' notion that a high P/E is a good thing, to refute the value investors' view that it means the company is overpriced. By comparing the P/E ratio with the projected earnings, you get a better idea of whether the stock is over or under priced. The PEG is simply calculated by dividing the P/E ratio by the projected annual earnings per share (EPS) growth. Many investors are now favoring this ratio over the simple P/E ratio.

The normal value of the PEG ratio should be one. This means the market is correctly valuing a stock according to its current earnings growth. A PEG ratio smaller than one implies the stock is undervalued, and the market is underestimating the growth potential. A PEG ratio larger than one suggests the stock is overvalued with excessive demand for shares or the market expects higher growth than the estimates.

The assumption with high P/E stocks might be they are growth stocks because investors are exhibiting a willingness to buy at a high price, which presumably means they feel the company has significant growth potential. The PEG ratio provides a check against that.

When looking at the PEG ratio, make sure you compare equals. For instance, it might be based on projected one-year growth or five-year growth, and the results will be different. However, it is a useful extension of the P/E ratio, and has been shown to be valid in many cases. The chief flaw is the emphasis on earnings growth because it is possible a company exhibits no growth in earnings but can increase cash flow, dividends, and other factors. The stock price can grow while the PEG ratio continues to show the stock as overvalued. It is probably best applied to growing companies rather than behemoths with established and stable returns.

The price/sales (P/S) ratio is another indicator investors use when valuing stocks. It measures the price of the company stock against the annual sales figures instead of earnings as the P/E ratio does. It reflects how much investors are paying for each dollar of sales, and some people feel it is a better indication because an accounting department can more readily manipulate earnings than recorded sales.

James O'Shaughnessy, in his book *What Works on Wall Street: A Guide to the Best Performing Investments Strategies of All Time*, calls the P/S ratio the "king of the value factors." He concludes "low price to sales ratios beat the market more than any other value ratio, and do so more consistently."

Finally, another parameter income investors value is the dividend yield, which is the amount a stock pays in dividends each year divided by the price of the stock. This is often calculated with the most recent quarterly dividend multiplied to give a per annum yield. Although income investors find this parameter important, growth investors tend to look toward capital gains and eschew such details. Whether a company pays regular dividends depends on the business the company is in and its stage of maturation. However, it is a matter of record that dividend-paying stocks have been better performers over the long term than stocks that do not pay dividends.

Stock indices

For those who wish to have exposure to the stock market, there are a range of stock indices available, each of which has different characteristics. The Dow Jones Industrial Average (DJIA), invented by Charles Dow, is one of the originals and is taken as a barometer of the American economy despite the fact it comprises the shares of only 30 companies. The values of the shares are weighted in the index to more closely provide a cross section of the economy, and on the rare occasion a company is substituted, it will come from an equivalent industry. General Electric (GE) is the only company that has been on the index since its inception at the end of the 19th century.

Other well-known U.S. stock indices are the S&P 500, the Russell 3000, and the NASDAQ 100, each of which is made up of the number of stocks contained in the name. Although these are the most popular ones, the Dow Jones company alone calculates more than 130,000 market indicators, including global indices and different sectors. However, only the major indices are readily tradable as such.

Whether looking at composite indices or at individual stocks, A solid portfolio will contain some U.S. equity exposure. From that starting point, you can look at the various sectors of the stock market to try to identify financial securities that can provide more diversification to the portfolio. The Standard and Poor's group divides stocks into 10 major sectors, which are:

- Basic materials
- Consumer discretionary
- Consumer staples
- Energy
- Financials
- Health care
- Industrials
- Information technology
- Telecommunications
- Utilities

Most of those categories are self-explanatory. Consumer discretionary includes Starbucks and Amazon. Other stock markets have similar sector divisions. When you are making up your portfolio, one of the basic strategies is to have a mix of these sectors to diversify your funds. During different phases of the economy, different sectors will do better than others. For instance, the consumer discretionary items benefit from good economic times whereas the health care and staples categories are steady performers even during the market's problems.

Within each sector, stocks are categorized by size, which is measured by market capitalization, or market cap for short. Market cap is the total stock value of the company, which is the share price multiplied by the total number of shares in the market. The market is split into three different sizes of company: large-cap, medium-cap, and small-cap. There are a couple of ways of dividing the companies into these groups, and they give similar groupings.

Large-cap companies are those with a market cap greater than $10 billion. Medium-cap companies go down from that to a market cap of $2 billion as a minimum. Small-cap companies are those that have fewer than $2 billion as a market capitalization. Small-cap sometimes is further divided into micro-cap and nano-cap for progressively smaller companies.

Another way of dividing the companies is to call the companies that make up 70 percent of all the money invested in the markets large-cap. The medium-cap is then made up of the next 20 percent. This leaves 10 percent of the total market capitalization for the small-caps. Despite only having 10 percent, these are much more numerous than the bigger companies.

The larger companies generally have a more stable stock price over time, and the small companies' shares are more likely to fluctuate. In general, this assessment means you are likely to have high returns from small-cap companies at the expense of higher risk. Some small-caps will disappear altogether, which is an unlikely event for the large-caps. Obviously, the varying level of risk is something to take into account when deciding on your asset allocation.

In addition to market sector and size of company, a third way of categorizing stocks is to talk about three different styles: value, core, and growth. These styles are subject to interpretation unlike the market capitalization division. Some information providers only include value and growth. The general principle is that growth stocks are in sound companies in markets that can look for steady progression; value stocks are theoretically somewhat underpriced, which is measured by looking at the P/E ratio. If the stock price is low relative to the earnings, which means the P/E ratio is low, it is seen as a sign the price could go higher. It is usual to compare the P/E ratio of companies similar in size and sector to find a fair value.

Because some stocks can qualify under both definitions, the distinction between value and growth is further confused. As a more subjective categorization, the style of stocks is less important than the company size or the market sector. If you are interested in exploring the stock market in more detail, a useful reference is the MorningStar website at **www.morningstar.com**. MorningStar is a mutual fund and stock research company that has developed a system for categorizing stocks called the MorningStar Style Box. This provides a useful reference when you are considering which companies to invest in.

Stock Mutual Funds

Most people are familiar with the concept of mutual funds. Mutual funds can provide another way to invest in equities, and the enormous range of mutual funds available means you can select virtually any market exposure you require. Mutual funds are regulated by the Securities and Exchange Commission, which provides legal protection, regulation, and restrictions on any companies that seek to offer a mutual fund to the public.

Many of the first mutual funds were closed-end funds, which means there were a limited number of shares for sale to investors. The shares, after the initial sale, were subsequently traded by the fund owners, who basically made the market for them. With a restricted number of shares, supply and demand created the pricing, which meant the price did not always reflect the value of the shares held by the fund.

Most mutual funds you will encounter are open-end funds. When additional investments are made in the fund, the fund buys additional shares to the same value. Open-end funds are only valued after the markets close, and the value is based on the value of the securities the fund holds divided by the number of shares the fund has issued. This is called the net asset value (NAV) of the mutual fund shares.

Investing in equities through mutual funds offers several advantages. Depending on the setup and goals of the fund, experts will select what they consider to be the stocks with the best potential performance, and because it is their job, you can expect them to be more knowledgeable and informed than you could hope to be. Another major advantage is the fund will be invested in a host of different companies, which provides better diversification than you might be able to achieve on your own.

Although mutual funds are not traded until after the markets are closed, when the NAV can be calculated, they are a liquid investment and allow you to buy and sell in any amount whereas stocks are best purchased in even lots. Mutual funds are available to invest in many financial instruments and provide the convenience many people prefer.

Some features of mutual funds are not so advantageous. You can choose a fund that does not make additional sales commission charges, called loads, and it is always in your interest to avoid these extra fees. However, you cannot avoid paying management fees, which might amount to at least 0.5 percent per year.

As with buying stocks directly, mutual funds will give you a choice of size and market sector. Although you can buy index funds that invest in all the companies contained in the index, it is easy to find funds that specialize in certain markets, such as energy or health care, and in types of investment, such as small-cap or value stocks.

International Investments

The global marketplace has many different asset classes, categories, and styles from which to choose. Although the United States currently holds more than 50 percent of the world's tradable securities, the percentage is decreasing each year. New securities are entering the market from emerging countries and becoming an important source for investors looking for different products. With new international securities, investors have more options for diversification, especially within the global market. The more international securities accessible to investors, the easier it will be for them to allocate a portion of their portfolios to global allocation and diversification. In addition, over the last few years, mutual fund companies have introduced several low-cost index funds.

With the number of stocks available on the U.S. markets, including international equities might seem to introduce further complication. However, including international stocks and funds in your portfolio can help with finding investments that are not as correlated and are better for your risk abatement. You can analyze the individual stocks in exactly the same way as domestic stocks although you might find some of the information more difficult to locate.

The fact that the stocks are based in other countries introduces several factors you do not find with U.S.-based stocks. International investing can be regarded as more risky than keeping your funds based in the United States for a number of reasons.

The first reason is the foreign currency risk. If the dollar strengthens against the currency you have invested in, your investment will perform poorly even if the stocks have nominally the same rate of return as your domestic stocks. However, because the dollar is weak during some periods, such as between 2013-1014, foreign currency risk can also work in your favor.

Depending on the country you are considering, you might find a political risk in holding stocks in that country. You are more likely to encounter this in less developed nations, but even developed nations can affect the value of your holding by government actions, such as imposing exchange restrictions on foreigners or introducing new regulations. One way to minimize these risks is to ensure the part of your portfolio held in the world markets is well-diversified so a political uprising in one country will have minimal impact.

Broadly speaking, international investments will be in one of two areas: developed markets or emerging markets. Developed markets, such as Germany, England, and Australia, have mature economies and are wealthy countries. Emerging markets are less developed and include countries Poland, China, Russia, and South Africa. Emerging markets contribute much less to the global economy and generally have higher risk and higher returns.

Because of the currency complications and the number of countries in which you should invest to diversify your portfolio, finding an investment fund that specializes in world investments is often a better idea than trying to buy individual equities. Funds are available to give you the exposure you want to the different markets and different sizes and sectors of company.

As you can see, stocks and stock funds can provide tremendous opportunities for investing in different marketplaces and with varying degrees of risk and return. The mere fact stocks are invested in different sectors does not mean they make a good combination for your portfolio because diversity is only part of the equation, which is what asset allocation teaches us.

Observe some general rules when managing a stock portfolio. These include not succumbing to overtrading to chase the latest fad. In most cases, you should develop a healthy skepticism toward anyone who claims to have a hot tip whether they are a relative, friend, or professional. By investing in stocks with strong fundamentals and keeping with the asset allocation strategies outlined in this book, you stand the best chance of keeping your portfolio in good shape.

Whomever you choose to help you with your stock selections, make sure you understand the different reasons for their advice and see any warning signs for yourself. Too often, it is the easiest course to hand over the responsibility for the selections to an expert. Then, you find out too late they were not as concerned for your account as you are. It is simpler to blame another person or adverse circumstances for poor performance than it is to accept that responsibility personally. It is your duty to yourself to keep track of your money. There will always be some winners and some losers, but with stocks, which will form the backbone of a reasonable investment portfolio, you should be able to watch your funds grow at a respectable rate.

It is much easier to buy stocks than to sell them. If a stock underperforms and loses money, liquidate it as soon as this becomes clear rather than hope for a turnaround. Although overtrading should be avoided, hope is rarely a good strategy in the financial markets, and avoiding catastrophic losses is part of good portfolio management.

In contrast to stocks, bonds are known as fixed income investments; although, as you will see in the next chapter, bonds can vary in value. However, bonds are generally considered to be a more stable and less exciting part of a diversified portfolio than stocks.

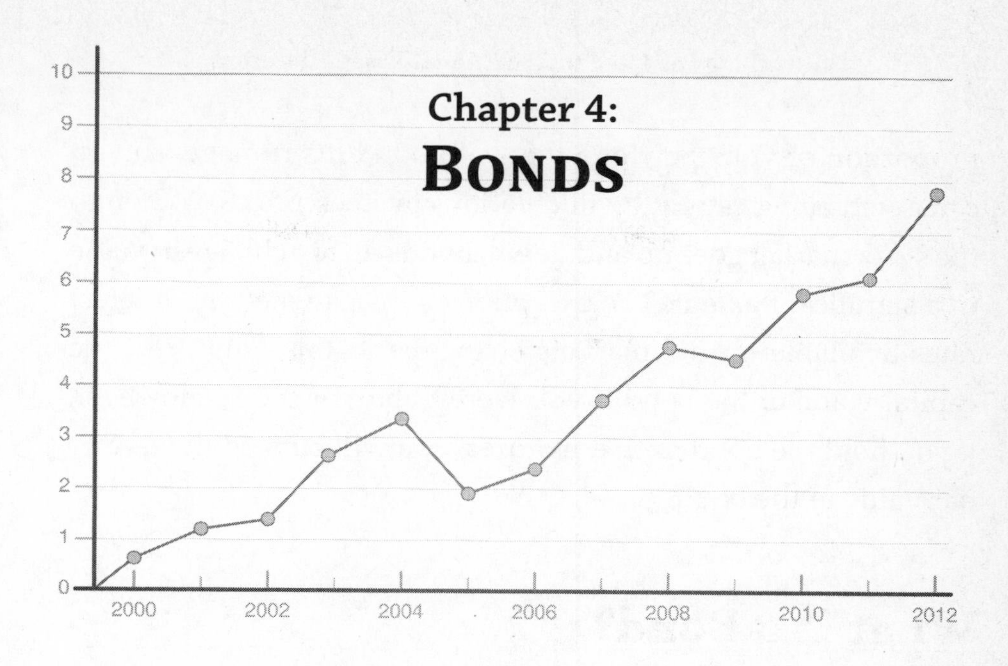

Chapter 4: Bonds

BONDS ARE FIXED INCOME INVESTMENTS. A WIDE VARIETY is available, including government bonds, investment-grade bonds, junk bonds, and asset-backed securities. You can also get a selection of bonds by choosing a bond fund. Although stocks and bonds are often mentioned together, a bond is a loan that will be repaid with interest, and a stock represents ownership in a company and can vary in value with the company's fortune. Bonds might also be issued for a specific purpose. A common example is when a school district issues bonds for specific school repairs and building projects.

In addition to providing a steady flow of income from interest payments, bonds have the advantage of not suffering from volatility to the same extent as stocks. However, they also offer a lower return on investment (ROI). If you are aiming for a specific financial goal in the near future, you might choose to increase the proportion of your portfolio that is in bond instruments so you can avoid being caught by fluctuations in stock prices. Although the stock market goes up and down, bonds do not change in value to a significant extent. The exception to this is when the interest rates available on the markets change, and this will affect the capital value of the bond if you were to buy or sell it. However, if you hold the bond until it matures, you will be paid the face or par value of the bond.

What is a Bond?

Those who invest in bonds have a different outlook and expectation to shareholders. The bond is money loaned to a company, organization, or government entity that must make regular interest payments to the investor and repay the loan on the expiration date. Even if the company has failed to make a profit, it is required to make the interest payments to bondholders and must borrow more money if necessary. Unlike with buying shares, the biggest risk the bondholder faces is the bond issuer will be unable to meet its financial obligations under the contract. This risk can be largely avoided by buying bonds of a high quality based on the rating systems that will be explained later.

The element of risk with bonds is slight and depends on who issues them. If they are government bonds, you can be fairly sure the obligations will be met at maturity even if the government needs to print more money to do so. If they are bonds a large-cap company issues, they are also fairly secure. If the bond issuer happens to default on the required payments, the bondholder has a better claim over any equity in the company than a stockholder.

The interest rate to be paid is predetermined and fixed. This might be called the coupon rate. This dates back to the days when a physical coupon would be printed and submitted for interest payment. The interest is paid at regular intervals, such as quarterly. For example, buying a $1,000 bond at a 4 percent interest rate will provide an investor with $40 annually or $10 for each quarterly payment.

Although the bond has a face value, it will not always change hands at that price if it is bought or sold before maturity. When the interest rates change, the market value of the bond will change depending on how it compares to the current rate. If interest rates rise, the investor can go elsewhere and buy a bond that will give a greater return; therefore, he or she would expect to pay less than the face value for an existing bond. This is called buying it at a discount. If the interest rates fall, an existing bond will become more valuable because of the comparatively high returns, and it will change hands at a higher price or premium. There are standard ways in which the discount or premium can be calculated to allow for the future value of interest payments, and investors frequently purchase bonds at a discount or a premium that relates to the prevailing interest rate and the coupon rate of the bond.

When you buy and hold a bond, you see the fluctuations in the bond's market value, which would increase or decrease. If you buy at a discount, you will receive the face value when the bond matures; if you buy at a premium, you still receive the face value at maturation, but it will be less compared to the purchase price. The key factor to bear in mind when you buy a bond at a premium or discount is how the interest rates on the bond relate to the current and expected market rates. If you buy a bond that is close to maturity, you will find the price is much closer to the face value regardless of the interest rate.

You can buy what is called a zero-coupon bond, which is a bond that has a coupon value of zero and pays no periodic interest. To compensate for this, the bond is available at a substantial discount to its face value, which makes it extremely attractive to investors who do not need regular income. This type of bond is frequently bought as a gift for a child and has a maturity date set for when he or she becomes an adult. The discount price on zero-coupon bonds is comparable to the amount a typical investor would earn in coupon payments by purchasing a bond at the standard market interest rate. Zero-coupon bonds make excellent savings vehicles for investors who are only interested in meeting long-range goals and do not require periodic payments.

One type of bond is generally not a good idea. This is a callable bond, which means the bond issuer can call in the bond at any time and simply pay back the value of the bond rather than wait until maturity. This makes it difficult for the investor to maintain a planned portfolio and can involve a substantial loss in revenue from coupon payments or in capital if the investor has bought at a premium.

Government bonds

There are two principal sources of bonds: government and corporations. The government category can be split into U.S. government and other types of government. The safest types of bond are those the U.S. government issues for the simple reason they are backed by the U.S. government, which is responsible for the money supply. The usual forms of U.S. government bonds are called Treasuries, and these are categorized into three types according to the time until maturity. The shortest term is a Treasury Bill, which matures within one year. Next are Treasury Notes, which go up to 10 years, and anything longer is known as a Treasury Bond, which can take as long as 30 years to mature. These bonds are extremely secure but subject to loss in value from inflation because interest rates are not high. The income generated is free of state and local income taxes, but it is subject to federal income tax.

Other types of bonds the U.S. government issues and backs include government agency issues, such as those issued by the Federal National Mortgage Association (FNMA), also known as Fannie Mae, and the Federal Home Loan Mortgage Corporation (FHLMC), also known as Freddie Mac. The U.S. government also backs certificates of deposit through the Federal Deposit Insurance Corporation (FDIC).

States and local governments issue the other type of government bond, often called a municipal bond or muni. These might be regarded as slightly less safe because of talk of states running out of money. However, the general obligation muni bonds are backed by taxes, so they have first call on the funds paid to the state, which fully backs them. The other type of muni bond is called a revenue bond and is issued by an agency or authority specifically to construct a project such as a turnpike or a hospital. This is still a low-risk loan, and the intention is the tolls charged for the turnpike or fees charged by the hospital will pay back the loan.

These muni bonds do not offer a high rate of interest, but their distinct advantage over higher-paying corporate bonds is they are free of state, local, and federal taxes. They combine excellent safety with a reasonable return, especially for investors who are in higher tax brackets and can benefit significantly from the tax advantages.

Corporate bonds

Corporate bonds generally pay more than government bonds, and they come in ranges of risk level and return. When a new company needs startup capital or an existing company needs funds for expansion, the corporate bond provides a way for private investors to help in return for prospects of higher returns.

The security of your money is only as good as the soundness of the issuing company, and you need due diligence to satisfy yourself in this respect. If the company goes out of business or enters into bankruptcy and the bondholder has some claim on the assets, there might be little or no return and it might take some time to recover any funds. Investing in a startup will be riskier than buying bonds a successful growing company needs to finance expansion.

You do not have to rely only on your own judgment about the risk involved with a higher return corporate bond. There are several series of grades various reputable rating companies issue that give you an assessment of the risk. The major credit rating agencies are Moody's, Standard & Poor's, and Fitch. Bonds are rated by investment grade and noninvestment grade, which gives an indication of the worthiness for long-term funds.

Investment grade bonds are rated BBB or higher by Standard & Poor's and Fitch, and Baa by Moody's. The best bonds are called Prime and attract three A's. Excellent bonds have two A's. Upper medium have a single A, and the lowest investment grades are called Lower medium. As implied by the names, these are the only types of bonds that you should consider for your portfolio because anything rated lower becomes too risky. The noninvestment grade bonds, or junk bonds, are speculative, and grades go down from BB, or Ba for Moody's. These are the types of bonds that offer returns similar to share investments, but you are exposed to much more risk than with other bonds. Of course, you would expect a good rate of return on these risky financial instruments, so you can gamble with nonessential money on them.

The level of risk also depends on time until maturity. If a bond only has one more year to run, the chance of default is less than if it were due in 10 or 15 years. If you buy a longer-term bond, check that the rating does not change during its term. If the rating falls, the value of the bond will likely diminish because other investors would expect a higher return for the perceived higher risk.

Which level of risk you find acceptable depends on your temperament and the way that risk fits into your asset allocation. Corporate bonds are more lucrative for investors because of the high yields they offer, but no company is immune from economic and market effects that can reduce trading and cause bankruptcy or other failure. Even a hostile takeover or an amalgamation might affect your investment. The final factor to consider is that interest payments from corporate bonds are taxable in federal, state, and municipal sectors, which can be a disincentive to some investors, especially those who already have a substantial amount of taxable income investments.

Bond mutual funds

Another way to invest in bonds is to buy bond mutual funds. These are mutual funds that invest in a variety of bonds, and you can select the type, including government, muni, or corporate; the length, including long- or short-term; and riskiness for corporate bonds. If you want to invest in junk bonds, a low-cost mutual fund that concentrates on such holdings is a good way to diversify the risk, and you have the advantage of an experienced manager doing corporate research, which gives you the best chance of a good selection.

Bond mutual funds give you a regular income from the investments in bonds and similar financial instruments. They generally pay dividends more frequently than the payments you would receive from buying individual bonds, and the returns are higher than those you would expect to see with money market and ordinary savings accounts. They include liquidity, stability, and diversification, which makes bond mutual funds popular for fixed income investing.

Bond mutual funds are also easier to buy than regular bonds because you can buy them like any other fund instead of going to a bond dealer. You can buy them in any amount instead of an even lot, and depending on the fund you pick, you have a measure of diversification built in. The only problem is there is no maturity date, so you won't know when you will receive the face value in return. There is no guaranteed value with bond mutual funds; whether the emphasis of the fund manager is short-term or long-term, value comes from buying and selling bonds to and from the fund on a rolling basis.

Bond mutual funds are likely to be the easiest way for investors to make a purchase in the fixed income markets. When you purchase bond funds, you are buying a share in a variety of individual bonds, which diversifies your holding and reduces the risk on any one particular bond in your portfolio.

Just as you can have international equities and invest in emerging markets to try for higher returns in exchange for higher risk, you can do the same with bonds. Countries are classified as developed markets and emerging markets for bonds in the same way for stocks. Emerging market bonds are higher risk and can be volatile because of the political considerations. To even this out, the first emerging market bond mutual funds were created in 1993, and these funds have done significantly better on average than the general bond index. The only year recently that emerging market has not performed better than the bond index was 1998, and this was because Russia defaulted on its foreign debt obligations. However, international bond mutual funds are subject to the same currency risk as all overseas investments.

CASE STUDY: FOCUSING ON LONG-TERM RETURNS

David M. Williams, CFP®
Wealth Strategies Group Inc.
8001 Centerview Parkway, Suite 201
Cordova, TN 38018
Phone: 901-473-9000

David Williams has consulted with businesses and their executives through his firm, Business Enhancement Associates LLC, since 2003. He helps business owners and corporations grow, protect, and transfer wealth. Williams is also an investment advisory representative with Advantage Investment Management Inc. Before establishing his business consultancy, he was director of financial planning for Regions Morgan Keegan Trust.

Williams has been a financial planner primarily for business owners since 1981. He has developed special expertise in advanced estate and charitable planning, employer stock option planning, and qualified plans.

Williams has been a Certified Financial Planner™ Practitioner since 1985. He is currently a mentor with Memphis Institute for Leadership Education (MILE) and was a president of the Financial Planning Association of the Mid-South. He is a co-author of the book Financial Savvy for the Small Business Owner *and is a regular contributor to* Transitions Magazine.

Asset allocation is important for individual investors to consider because it helps focus an investor on longer-term returns. It gives him or her a policy by which to compare and manage his or her portfolio. It also can help reduce downside risk of the entire investment portfolio.

One of the benefits derived from using an asset allocation strategy is reasoned discipline in the investment process. The goal of asset allocation is to provide the highest return for a specified degree of return volatility although it does not ensure a profit or protect against loss.

Asset allocation differs from diversification because it attempts to reduce systematic risk, or the tendency for investment prices to move together. Diversification attempts to reduce unsystematic risk, or risks associated with a specific security such as business and financial risk. Asset allocation looks at asset classes and their correlation. Diversification looks at the correlation of industries; form of ownership, such as bond or stock; and management of a specific investment. Diversification helps you spread risk throughout your portfolio, so investments that do poorly might be balanced by others that do relatively better. Neither diversification nor rebalancing can ensure a profit or protect against a loss.

Asset allocation fails to work when the asset classes being considered become highly correlated. For example, in 2008, international stocks, U.S. stocks, and bonds moved in correlation. In that environment, an investor who limited him or herself to traditional financial vehicles could not diversify away systematic risk because the universe of investments moved in sync.

When using an asset allocation strategy, an investor must consider it is not a static investment policy. As market conditions change, so does the correlation of asset classes. The blend of asset classes that diversify risk in one market could concentrate risk in other markets. The asset allocation will need to change to maintain a target risk/return profile.

The risk profile of the investors I work with matches their asset allocation strategy. That is the goal that I set before all my clients.

Assuming market conditions have not changed the correlation of asset classes, portfolio rebalancing restores a portfolio to its intended asset allocation mix. Returning the asset class balance when it drifts 10 percent from the target returns the portfolio to the targeted risk and return.

When I use asset allocation strategies with my clients, I often determine a client's perceived risk tolerance by analyzing the degree of volatility his or her current portfolio has. I use a mean-variance optimizer to determine an asset class allocation that maintains a similar degree of volatility with a return that lies along the efficient frontier. I then identify securities that provide a diversified proxy for the asset classes and then provide a plan to move the client's assets to the allocation.

> Asset allocation can hurt an investor's portfolio returns. In any measurement period, diversification and asset allocation guarantee you will get a lower-than-possible return. The highest return is achieved by concentrating all investment in the highest performing asset class or the highest performing security. This also accepts the highest degree of volatility. We cannot know what will be the highest performer in any period until after the period has passed.
>
> The efficient frontier is not an accurate indicator of investor expectations. No correlation is between the efficient frontier and investor expectations. The efficient frontier is a mathematical construct of highest return per degree of risk within the universe of asset class proxies. Investors expected to get 10 percent return with little downside risk with Bernie Madoff's asset management. Such a risk/return profile is outside of the efficient frontier in almost all market conditions.

Other fixed income investments

Although bonds are the most commonly discussed fixed income investments, they are not the only ones available. For the newcomer to the financial markets, bonds are the safest and easiest for a fixed income portion of your portfolio, but experienced investors will also look at the other following types.

Mortgage-backed securities

Mortgage-backed securities (MBSs) are based on a pool of mortgages that are used to pay income to investors. These can be risky, and in recent years the number of people defaulting on their mortgages has risen alarmingly, which has a direct impact on investing in mortgage-backed securities. The attractive side of investing in an MBS is the rate of interest you can receive, but the higher interest comes with higher risk. You can even choose to invest in higher-risk mortgages to gain higher potential interest.

With the current state of the economy and fluctuations within the financial community as a whole, it is essential to approach these investments cautiously. You can easily see the risk of these investments based on the record number of foreclosures during the foreclosure crisis of the last few years. Another problem with MBS investments arises when people prepay their mortgage instead of allowing it to go to term, in which case you receive your investment back but have to reinvest it at the current prevailing interest rate.

Collateralized debt obligations

Collateralized debt obligations (CDOs) or asset-backed securities are similar to the mortgage-backed securities, but they are much more general. They are backed by a variety of assets as collateral and not just real property. Even more than with an MBS, you need to research and know what you are getting into if you invest in a CDO. The backing assets can include bonds and loans, and these are your guarantee against default.

CitiGroup, Bank One and other companies offer CDOs on credit card receivables, and in this case, you need to understand how freely those credit cards were handed out because different issuers have varying criteria for offering credit. Similarly, GMAC and Ford offer auto loans that can be pooled together to give another type of investment vehicle. In this case, the assets can be seized in the event of default but not without some trouble and sometimes loss of value. Because motor vehicles are depreciating assets, the risk is high.

CDOs have been connected to subprime mortgages, so their popularity has declined significantly in recent years. Still, CDOs can be secured on many different assets, not just subprime mortgages. You can select the type of risk and have the opportunity of a higher return in exchange for higher risk. Many people consider CDOs as too risky for an investment portfolio and use them only as speculative vehicles.

Preferred stocks

Preferred stocks are included in this fixed income section because their characteristics are more like bonds than stocks. If you choose a preferred stock over a common stock, you lose the right to vote at the annual shareholder meetings, but in return, you have a higher claim on the assets than regular stockholders.

Preferred stocks pay a fixed dividend, which is paid the dividends of common shareholders if the company has financial difficulty. Like bonds, preferred stocks tend to have less capital appreciation than common stocks.

Convertible bonds

Convertible bonds are bonds that have stock options attached to them. Depending on the purchase agreement in force at the time the seller purchased the bonds, they can be converted into equity instruments by the buyer or the seller. They might be converted at the option of the buyer, or the seller might automatically convert them if the price of the stocks reaches a pre-assigned value. Although these bonds can provide a nice reward if the stock of the company increases substantially, they also have a lower yield than normal bonds you would buy from the same issuer.

Cash and money market instruments

Cash is a financial instrument that has been in circulation for centuries to pay for goods or services or to pay off debt. A cash equivalent is a short-term investment that is available for use in the near future. Cash and cash equivalents include cash, money market accounts, money market mutual funds, and certificates of deposit (CDs). Many people have cash or cash equivalents in their portfolios for one of two reasons:

- **Instant liquidity:** You can easily and quickly access cash from a checking account or savings account or from an investment account you have set up specifically to provide checking access as necessary. This is perhaps the best reason for holding cash or cash equivalents in your portfolio.

- **Stability:** Unlike other investments you might make, cash never varies from its face value. Even if the value of the dollar changes because of inflation, a $20 bill will still buy $20 worth of merchandise or services.

Stability is a good reason to keep cash in your portfolio, but unless you plan to make frequent withdrawals, you will lose more money than you gain. Over time, you will see the purchasing power of your money reduce. Short-term investments do not pay the same rate of interest you can earn on a long-term investment. Although these short-term investments are excellent choices for those who will need the funds for college and other short-term needs, they are not good choices for long-term investments because of their minimal returns.

For those who do not plan to make frequent cash withdrawals, you can receive the same stability by investing in short-term fixed income investments, such as bonds and bond funds. Although some bonds might be considered long-term investments, others, such as Treasury bills, mature in as few as 90 days. These instruments offer a better edge against inflation than cash although they might not provide the same return as long-term investments. However, they do offer fixed income, which is important to those who need additional cash for living expenses. Although cash might seem like a good idea, unless it is earning interest or bringing in a substantial return, it is not providing any protection against inflation.

Money market deposit accounts are popular investment tools partly because the cash is easily accessible. They provide the convenience of a standard checking account with higher interest rates. You will find some restrictions on withdrawals, but apart from that, they provide a nice return for those who choose to keep cash in a money market fund. The interest rates vary by a financial institution, but they are higher than the customary savings account. Some investors prefer these deposit accounts because they are controlled only by the interest rate the specific financial institution offers and tend to be less volatile than other financial instruments. Unlike other types of investments, the FDIC protects the money market account.

On the downside, the interest rates are subject to change at any time. They are related to the prime rate. In addition, the depositor must maintain a minimum balance or he or she faces stiff penalties up to and including closure of his or her account. The bank sets these minimum balances, which are connected to the interest rate. Most money market accounts have a minimum balance requirement of at least $1,000 although a few banks offer these accounts for smaller amounts.

In some cases, you might be able to link your checking or savings account to your money market account to save money on fees. Money market deposit accounts are excellent choices for those who have an additional deposit to make but do not wish to assume the risk of investing in the securities market.

In contrast to the money market deposit account, money market mutual funds are placed with a mutual fund company or through a bank or brokerage firm. This type of money market account is tied directly to your mutual fund account through the broker or mutual fund company with which you have your money market mutual fund account. This makes it convenient for an investor to receive his or her dividend and interest payments from other investments and proceeds from any sales of equities and securities. On the downside, the FDIC does not insure these particular money market accounts because they are not a typical bank deposit account. This means there can be more risk involved than with a standard money market account.

The money market mutual fund account is not intended to be a checking account, so the risks might not be of importance to the average investor. However, the risks are no more prominent than they are with an ordinary mutual fund account. There is always a risk the investor will experience a loss, especially if he or she is holding short-term investments. The mutual fund market generally can be less volatile than the securities market because of the constant movement of money among funds. Having a money market mutual fund account is a more convenient way to trade in the mutual fund market because it provides an easy way for an investor to transfer funds when he or she wishes to trade them. Although there are fees attached to these accounts, they are minimal.

Various financial institutions, including your bank, offer CDs, not to be confused with CDOs. You can find some of the most competitive interest rates by searching on the Internet, but do your homework carefully to ensure any issuing institution has substantial reserves. The FDIC covers many CDs, but if the FDIC has to step in and take over a bank, it can be difficult to access your funds when you want until the accounts are sorted out.

CDs are not as flexible as money market accounts because they include a clear commitment to leave the funds untouched for a certain time. Otherwise, you are charged a penalty. They pay a slightly higher interest rate, and you can choose the period for which your money is locked up. Longer-term CDs pay a higher interest rate. You can divide your money among different due dates so some cash is always available at short notice. If you don't withdraw the cash, you can roll the money into another CD. This is a process known as laddering.

Chapter 5: Alternative Investments

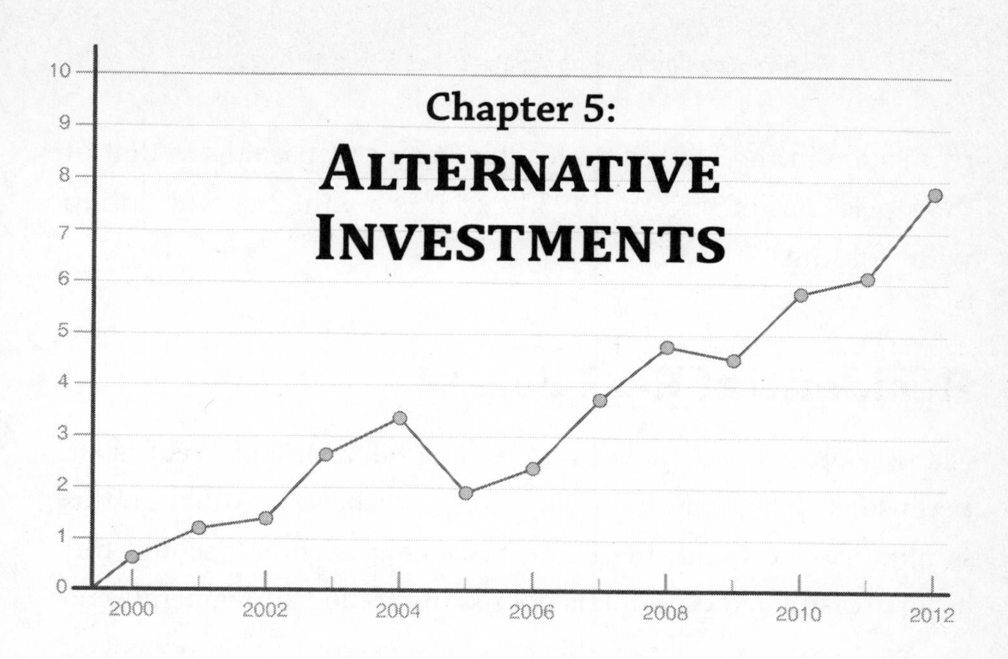

NO DISCUSSION OF INVESTMENT STRATEGIES WOULD BE complete without talking about real estate even though many people think of property ownership as separate from their portfolio. Whether the aspiration is to own a home or become a landlord, the decision to invest in property somehow is seldom related to portfolio management in a holistic manner. Including it in your asset allocation provides an asset class that has a low correlation to common stocks and bonds, and having assets that have low or negative correlation is useful in reducing the risk.

Investing in real estate does not mean you must become a landlord and deal with rental and maintenance issues. You can also conveniently invest in real estate by investing in publicly traded real estate investment trusts (REITs). If your portfolio is diversified with real estate in addition to stocks and bonds, you can look forward to superior performance. The rate of return on real estate in the United States has been comparable to that of the stock market since the 1930s, so it is a valuable addition to your holdings.

Residential Real Estate

Many people already have an investment in residential real estate because they own or are buying their own homes. Although this familiarizes you with the processes, many experts discount this as an investment because it is not readily traded and generates no income. Also, it is not possible to rebalance your portfolio as you are recommended to do periodically if your home is part of it.

Robert Kiyosaki, of *Rich Dad, Poor Dad* fame, has written several books about including real estate as an intrinsic part of your investments. He points out the tax advantages and various legal ways to avoid difficult tenants. As recent years have shown, there are financial risks in owning real estate, which discredits the popular myth that real estate always goes up in value. We have seen exactly the same story on the stock market, so real estate arguably is no worse an investment than equities.

Although it would be beyond the discussion of asset allocation to go into detail, real estate gives you the option of leveraging your money by buying rental properties with a mortgage. If the net income is sufficient to cover the repayments and all other costs, this can be a profitable plan. Whether you buy rental properties outright or use a mortgage, the net return is the important consideration.

If you are going to invest in real estate directly, you must be prepared to either do a great deal of work or pay someone to do it for you. Not everyone is cut out to be a landlord. If you are not competent at home maintenance, it is best to leave such things as repairing roofs, taking care of plumbing problems, and fixing heaters to maintenance staff. Investing directly in residential real estate can be profitable, but you should not buy a property with the expectation of easy profits.

Commercial Real Estate

Commercial real estate covers a wide variety of properties, including office buildings, warehouses, storage facilities, retail stores, malls, and even empty lots. Anything used for conducting business instead of for living is classified as commercial real estate.

If you are considering investing in real estate and are prepared to take on the problems and responsibilities that arise, it can be a good idea to invest in both residential and commercial real estate. Whether in the ease of finding a tenant, the amount of rent that can be charged, or the capital appreciation, one often lags behind the other, so having investments in both markets diversifies any fluctuations.

However, commercial real estate is a different proposition from residential rentals, and you should do your homework before venturing into the market. Direct investment in commercial property can lead to the best returns, but unless you have property management skills and knowledge of the real estate market, you might need to hire a management company to help you. This will reduce your returns. Perhaps the biggest problem is the illiquidity of the asset because when the time comes to rebalance or substitute an alternate asset, finding a buyer might be impossible.

Another way of investing directly in commercial real estate is through limited partnerships. The right partnership can be attractive. Because limited partners can have nothing to do with running the business, find a limited partnership with a good general partner. The general partner makes all the decisions for the partnership, including which properties to buy, how to manage them, and when to sell them. Limited partners are not allowed by law to be involved in these decisions. The liability of the limited partners is restricted to their investment, and a condition of this is they cannot be responsible for the partnership decisions. As with owning commercial property outright, this method of investing can be illiquid, perhaps even more than trying to sell a particular property onto the market.

Real Estate Investment Trusts

REITs are the simple way to take part in the real estate market. REITs are baskets of properties that trade on a stock exchange and provide instant liquidity. The company running the REIT takes care of buying, selling, and managing the properties in the trust's portfolio, so you can buy into the REIT and not worry about any other issues. The cost of management and administration can be a few percent. This detracts from the returns on your investment but is the cost of getting rid of the headaches.

REITs were originally designed as a tax efficient way of owning a selection of properties. The company managing the REIT is exempt from federal and state income tax although it does need to comply with Internal Revenue Service guidelines to maintain this exemption. The main requirements are that it pays dividends of at least 90 percent of the taxable income to the shareholders, it invests at least 75 percent of your assets into real estate, and it derives at least 75 percent of its income from the real estate rents.

The original legislation to allow REITs was written in 1960, but they have only become popular during the previous couple of decades because of other law changes. They offer both income and long-term growth with relatively high returns. The dividend pays better than most equities, and the income largely is predictable because REITs invest in commercial property for which long-term leases are the rule.

REITs invest in commercial property in two main ways. The first way is called the equity REIT, which invests directly in real estate and owns the property. The second way is called the mortgage REIT, which provides funds for commercial mortgages but does not take direct ownership unless there is a foreclosure. This is similar to mortgage-backed securities. You can also find a hybrid REIT that combines both of these investment types.

There are about 100 different equity REITs to choose from in the U.S. markets, and you can also buy a mutual fund that combines the results of many REITs to diversify your investment. REITs have generally increased in value at about the same rate as the stock market but have progressed independently. At one stage, they even showed a negative correlation, which makes them good candidates for a diversified asset allocation strategy.

Commodities

Despite the fact most people think of other asset classes when they consider their investment portfolio, you can invest your money in a number of other items with a reasonable expectation of either income, capital growth, or both. Commodities are one of the riskier asset classes and therefore are not recommended except for speculation.

Investing in commodities brings variety to your portfolio. Commodities are common items: agricultural products, including sugar, corn, and wheat; basic materials, such as steel and copper; energy assets, including oil, gas, and electricity; and precious metals, such as gold and silver. Prices of commodities vary with the supply and demand, and with few exceptions, the producers will explore, mine, or grow more over time if the demand rises.

There are two ways to invest in commodities. One of them is to trade the actual commodity, and the price at which it is bought and sold is called the spot price. The other way is to trade futures, and the price in this case is for delivery of the commodity at a specified date in the future. The investor might not be interested in the spot price for some of the commodities. Agricultural goods, in particular, are perishable and can be bulky, so you are unlikely to hold a ton of wheat with the hope of capital appreciation. On the other hand, you might buy some ounces of gold, keep them in a safety deposit box, and expect the price to rise. On balance over time, gold investors have earned at the rate of inflation, which is hardly surprising when you consider that inflation is just a measure of the devaluation of paper money.

Apart from the risk of deterioration, commodity storage could be a problem, so most large investments in commodities are made through the purchase of commodities futures contracts. These are contracts in which investors, traders, producers, manufacturers, and any other interested parties agreed to buy or sell the assets in question at a later date for a predetermined price. Buying and selling futures contracts allows investors to take advantage of the change in price of a commodity without having to possess it.

Few investors have investments directly in the futures market. Instead of buying futures directly, they purchase them through mutual funds, exchange-traded funds (ETFs), or exchange-traded notes. This form of commodity investing can take place on a stock exchange, just as with equities, and is the easy way to benefit from any change in price. Futures contracts have a pre-established size and a date for delivery and can be less convenient than these methods.

Some funds concentrate on the one particular type of commodity, such as gold, while others are made up of a variety of commodities. Unless you are prepared to research and develop expertise in commodities, the wisest course is to focus your commodity investments on baskets of commodities instead of trying to pick specific ones. Index funds are available that are designed to repeat the possible return from a basket of commodities, and these would diversify your investment and spread the risk. In practice, they combine the price movement of commodities, the difference between futures contracts expiring on different dates, and income from Treasury bills.

The reason you have income from Treasury bills is that futures contracts can be bought on margin. The index assumes the margin requirement, 5 percent, is paid for the contract, and the remainder of the value is invested in Treasury bills. The total return index fund therefore reflects this strategy.

Commodity funds are attractive to investors because they have a low correlation to stocks and bonds, which make up a major part of the portfolio. The less attractive part is that commodity total return indices have low returns and low correlation. Although desirable, this cannot by itself create a fair return. For this reason, commodities are not popular with investors.

Exchange-Traded Funds

ETFs are a fairly recent idea in the markets compared to mutual funds. They are similar but have certain distinct differences. ETFs are registered with the Securities and Exchange Commission (SEC), and each fund contains a selection of securities just like a mutual fund. The major difference between an ETF and a mutual fund is that, as the name implies, an ETF can be bought or sold on a stock exchange whenever the exchange is open for trading.

ETFs have become popular, and the number of ETFs available is increasing and covering all areas of the market. A mutual fund is only priced at the end of each day, and the price, called the net asset value (NAV), is directly and exactly calculated from the closing prices of the securities in the fund. In contrast, because the ETF is bought and sold throughout the day, the price can vary by the influence of supply and demand and does not have to completely reflect the underlying securities' values.

Many ETFs are considered passively managed and simply reflect the movements of an index most easily by investing in the shares of the index. Other types of ETFs include negatively correlated funds, which means when an index goes up, the fund value goes down and vice versa, and ETFs that multiply the index movement, which means the fund value goes up twice as much as the index goes up. These types of ETFs require sophisticated management to achieve those objectives. The fees and expenses associated with exchange-traded funds are lower than those you will encounter with many mutual funds.

A final difference between the ETFs and mutual funds is that, because they are traded on a market, they can be bought on margin and sold short. Buying on margin means you do not pay the full value for the fund or equity you trade but instead pay interest to the broker for the difference you have borrowed. A stockbroker will allow you a 50 percent margin for equities, so you only have to put down half the value. Selling short, as with shares, means you can profit from a fall in the value of the fund.

CASE STUDY: DETERMINING YOUR TOLERANCE FOR RISK

James Williams
Lincoln Financial Advisors
20 Thicket Lane
Lancaster, PA 17602
Phone: 717-669-6188
james.williams3@lfg.com

James G. Williams provides retirement, post-divorce, and estate planning services and related insurance and investment services for individuals, their families, and privately held businesses.

Williams continues to serve the clients he established during his 14 years in the financial services profession and is also accepting new clients.

Williams holds the title of financial planner and maintains his Series 7, 63, and 66 securities registrations along with the life, health, and annuity licenses. He is a member in good standing with the Financial Planning Association, the National Institute for Certified College Planners, the Ancient Order of Hibernians, the Knights of Columbus, and the Southern Lancaster County Chamber of Commerce.

Asset allocation is extremely important and relevant for individual investors to consider because every investor and their level of sophistication with investing is different. Some can afford to be much more risk-averse than others. To determine someone's tolerance for risk at any given period in his or her life, administer a suitability questionnaire.

Once the results of the questionnaire are known, a portfolio can be constructed that allots investments to the style determined by the questionnaire. For example, if an investor is not immediately concerned with receiving or reinvesting income derived from an investment, he or she tends to be more growth-oriented, and their asset allocation would be made up of mostly stocks that do not pay dividends. If income is important or if volatility is a major concern, the allocation should be constructed to include dividends and interest as a byproduct of the investment.

Asset allocation should be conceived as a schematic or design of what an investor hopes to build over a period of time. It should allot for short-, medium-, and long-term goals where appropriate. Proper asset allocation should divert a measure of risk away from the investor by not allowing him or her to be overweighted in one investment vehicle over another.

Asset allocation is extremely helpful in diversifying an investor out of a large concentrated stock or bond position and into prudent or risk-averse portfolios depending on the investor's tolerances for such.

There can be many benefits from using an asset allocation strategy when the tool works. There have been a lot of recent discussions suggesting there was no safety regardless of how well an investor was diversified across investments in their asset allocation. Therefore, a key benefit within a properly allocated portfolio was lost unless, of course, that allocation was more income- or cash-oriented at the time of the market's most recent pullback in 2008.

Again, one of the key benefits to an asset allocation strategy is in its ability to mitigate or appropriate some level of risk.

Though similar in context, asset allocation and diversification differ in what they bring to the investment picture. For example, consider asset allocation the blueprint of a mixed-use office building with seven floors.

This building will have retail space on the first and second floors, traditional office space on floors three through six, and flexible space on the seventh floor. The purpose for this building is to bring a little something different to a moderately populated urban area that is seeing a new cycle of growth due to recent expansions to a local college.

The builder chose a location that was accessible from almost any direction with the hope of attracting many suitable tenants. To avoid overlap of the goods and services offered within this one venue, a property manager is hired to sort through the interested potential tenants to make sure there are not too many of the same types of businesses. In this way, the building's owners could mitigate the risk that their building would become like all of the others in town and eventually perform less than expected.

The property manager then set about the task of filling the first two floors with a quaint pub, an alternative foods restaurant, a small tea room, medium-sized nationally or regionally known clothing boutiques, and a specialty sporting goods store. One bank, an insurance company, and a law firm filled the office space, and the building's architect and engineering firm filled the sixth floor. A spa and pilates studio took the seventh floor. Many buildings are developed with one tenant in mind, but the owner runs the risk of developing a space that will only ever be able to fit one business. Another type of business might require all sorts of special needs to retrofit the space for its purpose. If a suitable tenant is not found, the owner runs an even greater risk of losing the opportunity of sustainable growth or income. In our example, the developer knew of this inherent risk and did not ever want to be in the position of putting all of their hopes on one type of business to sustain them. Instead, they diversified their building space to attract and maintain a mixture of steadily growing companies and provide them with renewable income in an attractive and sought-after space.

The purpose of this example is to show the importance of diversification across many asset classes, or floors and business types, within one asset allocation.

During the 2008 market crash, we believed a well-allocated portfolio, invested for the long term, would shield investors or, at minimum, soften the ride downward. In this market event, there was no safe haven other than cash and U.S. Treasuries. Even though many companies have lived through the downturn, the herd mentality is what leads many fearful investors to liquidate their strategy sooner than they need to. Time in the market will often reap greater benefits than trying to time the market. Asset allocation is the foundation of fundamental investing. Fundamental investing is essentially the buying and selling of an investment when earnings and management are doing well and when they are not.

Technical investors look for buy and sell signals that are mostly based on the volume of a stock or a bond's sells and buys and whether new lows or highs are turning into a pattern. Technical investors live and hunt on Main Street and on Wall Street. It is the technical trading, speculating, or betting that continues to challenge Modern Portfolio Theory, the efficient frontier, and a solid asset allocation.

The following are items the investor should consider when using an asset allocation strategy:

- Which level of risk am I comfortable with accepting when considering how to weight the asset classes I will be invested in?
- How will I determine the most opportune time to rebalance the allocation back to its mean, for example, 50 percent equities, 35 percent bonds, 10 percent REITs, and 5 percent alternatives?
- Will I be the only person accountable for my success, or will I hire a co-fiduciary?
- Which price am I willing to put on that advice, or how much will I pay for assistance?
- Is my allocation meeting or exceeding its purpose? If so, should I change it, and when?

The risk profile of the investors we work with does not always match their asset allocation strategy. It depends on the point at which the assessment is taken in the planning process and subsequent allocation implementation. Although my preference is to perform some level of financial planning before recommending an investment program, if planning preceded my involvement, I would at a minimum administer a suitability questionnaire to determine an appropriate risk-adjusted allocation. I do not ever want to be in a situation in which the investor questions the appropriateness of an allocation; I insist they sign off on any recommendation I make only after they can demonstrate they understand it.

Portfolio rebalancing will only work when the investor accepts its necessity. The needs of the investor and his or her appetite for risk will naturally change over time, so today's asset allocation might need a complete overhaul 10 years from now. It will definitely need to be re-examined as the investor nears a particular event in his or her life, such as early, mid, or late retirement.

Investors often ask about including alternative asset types within their original allocation, such as oil and gas, REITs, commodities, and currency. If the asset type is appropriate for their risk tolerance, add it. Once this happens, though, the purity of the original allocation has been altered and the mean has to be reset.

Every one of my clients has a different set of goals, dreams, and desires. I work to help them ascertain those goals. After determining their risk tolerance, I create an asset allocation or schematic that is based on the Modern Portfolio Theory training I received many years ago. First, I account for any existing investments and, where appropriate, incorporate them into an asset mix.

For example, if I had a client who wanted to participate in the market and had a large position in the company stock of a former employer but wanted less volatility in a portfolio, I would create a mix of large-cap, mid-cap, small-cap, and international growth or value stocks. This design holds true for a portfolio of mutual funds, which is a preference of mine. Additionally, the questionnaire indicates an approximate time frame of when the funds will be needed. The shorter the time frame, the more income-oriented the investments generally will be although this is not a steadfast rule.

For this example, the client would feel most comfortable investing 50 percent in stocks, 40 percent in bonds or CDs, and 10 percent in real estate investment trusts. An asset allocation or mix with only 50 percent in equities is generally considered to be balanced. Professional portfolio managers are often at odds over which mix makes an allocation balanced, but the mix mentioned above is at least accepted in concept.

This balanced allocation is designed to give the client market participation with a cushion to fall on during volatile markets.

A carefully implemented portfolio allocation should, over the time frame and purpose the client needs the investment, provide consistent returns, not hurt a portfolio. Often, when investors get jealous of what their neighbor and relative claim they are getting from their investments, the investors will succumb to the temptation and stray from the allocation to chase a return for which the risk is unknown. If an investor's risk profile suggests he or she can only handle moderate swings of volatility, he or she should stay the course. Pulling up stakes before a plan is realized as fruitful might cause unrecoverable damages. Proper asset allocation is a design method that often protects investors from their innate fears and greed.

Asset allocation in one account or across an investor's many accounts should be purpose-driven. If they have play money they do not mind losing, allocate a small percentage away from the goal-oriented portfolio to avoid hurting the short-, medium-, and long-term intentions.

The efficient frontier is not an accurate indicator of investor expectations relative to risk versus returns; however, it is a good tool to help an investor gauge where they are most comfortable on the risk versus reward scale for each concentration, or scaled increment, of the mix of stocks to bonds and fixed income.

Derivatives

Do not be scared by the name derivative and the connotations it has of mathematics and calculus. The financial derivative is just something that derives its value from something else. In other words, you are not buying the something else directly. You are buying something that varies in price according to something else. Most derivatives have time constraints and are therefore not suitable to hold unattended in a portfolio. Most derivatives also leverage your money, which means you can win or lose much more than you stake.

Despite the fact you probably will not look directly for derivatives for your investment portfolio, they can be useful for hedging purposes.

Futures

For traders, futures offer an exceptional opportunity for profit, which must be balanced against the risk involved. The futures contract is simply a binding contract to buy or sell something at a future date. The price is agreed, and if appropriate, quantity and quality are set. The futures contract is a derivative because any value it has as the contract is derived from something. Only later will the actual goods change hands for money in compliance with the agreed transaction.

One of the reasons futures were invented was to help farmers control their costs and predict their income without suffering wild fluctuations. Farmers could know in advance how much they would be paid for their crop or livestock when they sold it six months later. This would allow them to plan their expenses and even to switch to another crop if they thought it would give better returns.

The other party to this particular futures contract could be a cereal manufacturer who might control and regulate his or her costs and secure a supply of grain at a set price for future production. Both the farmer and the manufacturer would feel they had gained from having a predictable future, so neither would be concerned if the market price when the transaction was done were different from what they had agreed.

Neither the farmer nor the manufacturer would purposely put themselves out of pocket. The price they agreed to at the outset was one they were both happy with, so the futures contract has no built-in disadvantage. It is only when it appears the price will be higher or lower than the market price that the contract gets its value.

Wherever there is the prospect of money to be made, someone will try to do so. If there is a bumper crop and the actual price drops, the farmer's contract to sell at a certain price will become more valuable; if there is a drought and the price of grain goes up, the cereal manufacturer's contract takes on a positive value. Therefore, futures contracts can be traded for significant amounts sometimes.

You can look at the price in two ways: the price of the goods and the time value, or the value for the time until the date the content must be settled. Some futures contracts are easy to value. With a futures contract on gold, which does not deteriorate, the seller in the contract could simply borrow money to buy the gold now and pay interest until the settlement date. This way of calculating a value is called cash and carry. If the contract were worth more than the current price plus interest, the seller would make money without any risk. Everyone would do that until the price came down, which effectively sets a maximum on what the price of the contract could be.

You have futures contracts on many different things, including commodities. The thing is called the underlying or underlier because it is the basis of the contract. The underlying can be a solid physical item, such as gold, bacon and other perishable agricultural goods, or even single stocks or stock market indices. The futures contract is still based on what value these things attained by the expiration date of the contract.

Futures contracts are a commitment to a transaction in the underlying at the future expiration date. You can buy and sell futures contracts before they expire because they will change in value over time, and this is how futures speculators make a profit. Some contracts have actual physical deliverables, but most traders do not let the contract reach the point at which they have to take delivery. Other contracts are always settled in cash; for instance, if you had a futures contract on a stock market index, you would not receive a cash adjustment on the delivery date, not stocks. You can look up the rules for settlement of what you decide to trade and the standard dates for expiration of the contracts.

Futures are not the only way you can commit to buying and selling something in the future. They are standardized with a specified quality and quantity of goods and a certain date, but before futures, there was a similar trading tool called a forward contract. A forward contract was specifically written to suit the two people agreeing to it. Everything, such as the amount of goods and the quality, would be written in the contract. Forward contracts are still used for specific requirements but generally not traded like futures contracts.

Because futures contracts have been standardized, the market for them is highly liquid, and they are easily traded. They are traded through an exchange, which means performance is guaranteed, and you do not need to worry about the credit worthiness of the other party.

The reason people trade futures contracts instead of simply trading equities is because of leverage, which multiplies the power of your money. Because you do not pay for the goods before the delivery date but only put up a small percentage to take out the contract, futures contracts are attractive to traders looking to make large sums of money on the markets. However, the leverage can work against you if the contract falls in value, and you can end up owing more than your original stake, which is why some people think futures contracts are dangerous.

One point to note is "marking to market." Each day, your broker will review the contracts you hold and update their value according to the current market price of the contracts. This means the value of your account varies every day. If your account loses too much value, your broker will ask you to deposit more money to protect him or her against suffering any losses. This is called a margin call, and you have to respond to it within a short time. If you do not answer it, the broker is allowed to do whatever is needed to protect him or herself from loss, which might include selling the futures contracts and any other financial securities held in your name.

On the other side, if your contracts are increasing in value, your account grows daily even though you have not closed any trades.

Options

If you like the idea of the leverage you get with futures but are worried about the possibility of losses running away with you, there is an alternative called options. Options, at least if you buy them, give you the option to buy or sell something at a certain point in the future. They are like futures contracts in that there is an underlying and a delivery date. They are also unlike futures contracts because there is no commitment to go through with the deal and you will only exercise the option if it will make you a profit, so you do not have to fulfill the contract if you would lose more money. Because you have this option, or choice, you must pay for the privilege, and you therefore have to buy an option. What you pay for the option, the premium, is money that will not be returned.

Of course, if you run the option through to the delivery date, you need to make a profit on the underlying price before you break even on the whole deal. After that, your potential gains are not limited while your downside is already paid.

You have many choices when you trade options. You can pick the price you want for the underlying — the strike price — and you can choose the expiration date — the strike date — from a range of dates. These factors will affect how much you pay for the option.

Options can be referred to as in the money, at the money, and out of the money depending on the price of the underlying compared with the option contract price. If the strike price is the same as the underlying price, the option is at the money. If the strike price is less than the current price of the underlying, the option is in the money, which means you would make a profit. If the strike price is more than the current price, you are out of the money. These relationships apply for a call option, in which you have bought an option to buy the underlying in the future. You can also buy a put option that gives you the right to sell the underlying at a certain price in the future, and the reverse relationships would apply.

The put option equates to going short on shares and gives you a profit if the underlying price falls. It works in exactly the same way as the call option by giving you the right but not the obligation to sell the underlying at the expiration date at the strike price. In this way, you can make a profit in a rising or a falling market as long as you anticipate the direction correctly.

Using options limits your risk to the premium you paid while giving you an upside with no limit. This is the way many people use them, but you can also take on more risk and be the seller of options. You will take the premium in return for taking that risk.

When you already own the shares and therefore would not be open to big losses if you had to surrender them to the option buyer, your strategy is called a covered call. This means you are covered if the option buyer calls the shares away from you. If the price does not change in favor of the buyer, you can sell another call option after expiration and keep doing this to generate a regular income. As long as you choose your option price carefully, the shares might never be called away from you, and you can continue to enjoy the income.

It is also possible to do this selling a put option, and some traders use this strategy if they want to buy some shares at slightly less than the current price. By selling the put option at the price you are prepared to pay, the worst that could happen is you receive the premium and you have to buy the shares at the price you wanted. If the share price does not fall by the expiration date, you have received the premium as a bonus and can sell another put option at the price you want to pay.

Contracts for difference and spread betting

The Securities and Exchange Commission does not permit contracts for difference (CFD) derivatives in the United States, but they are widely available around the world, including in England and Australia. Contracts for difference allow you to take out a contract on virtually any underlying financial instrument and profit from the difference in price of the underlying over time. Because you do not have to buy the underlying financial security, these again leverage your funds, and you only put down a small percentage to enter the contract.

For those who are eligible to buy CFDs, they can be an efficient way to trade. Whenever shares change hands in the U.K., there is a stamp duty to be paid, and when you buy something and sell it for a profit, it is customary to be charged capital gains tax (CGT) on your profit. Using CFDs to trade on the stock market avoids both these penalties. Because you do not own the underlying financial instrument at any time, at no point can stamp duty be charged, and in a similar way, the profits are not technically capital gains, which avoids CGT.

Spread betting is similar to CFDs in its tax avoidance. Again, it is not available in the United States, but it is becoming popular in the U.K. and other countries that allow it. Unlike in the United States, gambling winnings are not taxed in the U.K., so this type of financial derivative, which can be called betting, is free of penalty.

The spread better can place a bet, such as £1 per point, on many different underlying financial figures, such as the FTSE 100 index or the S&P 500 index. Spread betting can also occur on sporting events, which is outside the scope of this book. The bet can be for the index to rise or to fall, and a slightly different value is assigned to each. This is the spread of the better, which turns out to be the way the dealer makes a profit.

For example, if the spread better was interested in trading the FTSE 100 index, the dealer might quote the two prices: 5989.0 and 5991.0. This means you can place a bet the price will go up, or buy, at 5991.0, or you can sell at 5989.0 and bet the price will fall. To close the bet, you must do the opposite, so this is where the dealer or bookie makes the amount of the spread.

This is simple betting in which the better never has an opportunity of owning the underlying, so the spread better avoids stamp duty and capital gains tax as with CFDs.

For a trader interested in short-term gains, CFDs and spread betting offer several advantages over simple share trading, not least of which is the leverage or gearing of your money. Although, recognize that this leverage can work against you to magnify any losses. For a long-term portfolio, they can be used to temporarily hedge positions and allow you to retain ownership of your investments and avoid loss even when you believe they might lose money in the short term.

For instance, suppose you believe in the long-term future of some oil shares you have, but you can see there might be a temporary setback or retracement in the price for political reasons. Rather than sell the shares to avoid the loss and have to realize any capital gains you had, on which you would be taxed in the current year, you could keep your portfolio and bet against the shares with a spread bet. In this case, you would sell because you believe the price will fall in the short term.

If you are right, your spread bet will compensate for the loss even though your shareholding loses value as the share price drops. If you are wrong, you will lose on your spread betting position, but you will receive capital gain on the shares. If the price does not change, you will simply lose the spread on your bet; this is the cost of hedging your position and it essentially is like an insurance premium. In countries that permit CFDs and spread betting, they can be handy tools to use in conjunction with your investments.

Hedge Funds

You might also consider investing in a hedge fund if you are qualified. This is a sophisticated pool of investments you might not be privy to as an individual. As a pooled investment, it is similar to a mutual fund, but if you have been watching the news, you know hedge funds can make significantly more profit or crash and burn. This is because of the way the hedge fund is set up. The manager of a hedge fund has a lot more freedom than a mutual fund manager because the level of regulation is much lower. The manager can invest in virtually any type of financial instrument he or she believes will be profitable. The only criteria is the manager follows other laws on taxes or fraudulent or criminal activity.

So, why do most investors not consider hedge funds? Quite simply, the hedge funds' lack of regulation is allowed because they are restricted to what are considered sophisticated investors. The regulations are in place to protect the common investor, but if the investor meets the requirements of a high net worth or annual income, the SEC considers him or her to be an accredited investor and therefore qualified to take care of his or her own investing decisions. Some regard it as a loophole in the law.

Many financial advisors will encourage investors to include real estate and even commodities in their portfolios but not recommend hedge funds. Hedge funds have traditionally attracted high fees for the managers and therefore are totally dissimilar from the mutual fund market in which competitive fees are a factor. Dramatic fund performance is the chief criterion by which accredited investors will select the fund to invest in, and the minimum investment can be a significant amount. With most funds imposing strict limits, they are also not easily withdrawn. The elaborate trading strategies hedge fund managers might become involved with are not easily unwound, and the sudden withdrawal of funds can be detrimental to the fund as a whole.

There are many different hedge fund strategies, including using short selling, derivatives, and specially arranged deals that are not open to the typical investor because of the amount of money at the hedge fund manager's disposal. The hedge fund manager might be ranked by the alpha he or she can generate in the fund, which is a technical measure of the fund's performance. The manager is able to implement strategies to make money from virtually any market action up, down, or sideways. In this way, the advantage over mutual funds is considerable.

Following are some of the categories of hedge fund strategies you might see. Many hedge fund managers will use several different strategies as the market changes, but the hedge fund is focused on a particular way of making a profit.

One strategy known as the long/short equity strategy involves the fund manager in basic stock market prediction. The stocks that are believed to go up in value are traded either by owning the stock outright or by purchasing a call option on it. Stocks that are expected to go down can be sold short or a put option purchased. It is also possible to sell a call option and receive the option premium with no expectation the option will be exercised.

Another strategy, which is in contrast to trading on simple equities, is the global macro strategy. It requires managers to focus on whole sectors and regional markets. Instead of trading securities, the fund manager might take positions in futures markets, either long or short, and in other derivatives. For instance, if the manager expects the U.S. stock market to perform better than the Japanese market, he or she might buy U.S. stock market index futures and sell short Japanese stock market index futures. The fund manager does not deal with individual equities and prefers to use derivatives for their leverage.

There are whole class of hedge fund strategies that come under the umbrella of arbitrage, which basically means buying an asset cheaply in one market and selling it straightaway for profit in another market. Outside of the financial world, this is a technique many entrepreneurs have used on eBay. When someone flips real estate, they are exercising arbitrage. Arbitrage opportunities do not last long because traders taking advantage of them tend to correct the market differences, but in many circumstances they give certain profits rather than speculative ones.

Some investors like the idea of spreading their hedge fund investments over several different strategies. Achieving this can be quite difficult, particularly when you consider the minimum investment requirements many hedge fund managers impose. Nonetheless, many investors feel they do not have sufficient investment expertise to choose which strategy will perform best, and it is usual for the hedge fund to restrict how readily you can withdraw funds, which you must do to put them into another investment.

One answer to this is the fund of funds (FOF), which combines investments in several different hedge funds. The mix of strategies is decided by the FOF manager. It might change over time as different opportunities come up, so the individual investor has little say on which strategies the money is pursuing. The FOF is one recourse when the investor cannot decide which fund strategy to invest in and the manager is researching opportunities full time, so this might not be a problem.

One issue with the FOF is it adds another layer of management fees to the already high hedge fund manager fees. These are in the range of two and 20, which means a 2 percent flat fee on the amount that is invested and a 20 percent charge on the profits the manager generates. The FOF manager's fee would be in addition to this.

It is expensive to invest in hedge funds, and they have a further disadvantage in that your money is locked in by contract, which makes it unavailable for other purposes or able to be rebalanced. The FOF might have a minimum investment of $25,000, but hedge fund investments require many times this amount and therefore are not for the novice investor. Currently, the Securities and Exchange Commission requires an individual to have income exceeding $200,000 for the past two years, a couple to have joint income more than $300,000, or an individual to have a net worth of $1 million. If you only meet these minimums, it is unlikely you should consider investing in a hedge fund for the simple reason that it would be a major part of your portfolio and not permit diversification or reasonable asset allocation.

Collectibles

Alternative assets can help lower risk levels and increase the portfolio return because they have a low correlation with the traditional investments. The most enjoyment perhaps can be had from investing in collectibles, such as artwork, rare coins, and wine, and many of these have proven to be excellent investments. However, you might want experts to evaluate some of the alternative investments, and some, such as art, are not easily bought and sold, which gives you an illiquid investment that is hard to rebalance with the rest of your portfolio.

Anything that can be bought with the prospect of increasing value can be included in this class of assets. Unlike a mutual fund, some collectibles can be financially rewarding and also enjoyable to collect and look at. The items traditionally considered to be collectible include stamps, coins, antiques, and fine art. Anything rare, unusual, or even unique can be considered a collectible item. An example of something more recent is an original handwritten score for a Beatles song. It is not within the purview of this book to advise on such purchases, but if you have expertise and the passion for a particular field, it is possible to include consideration of such items within your portfolio.

If you do consider including collectibles within your portfolio, take into account the illiquidity of many of them. Liquidity is important to many investors, and the more liquid the asset is, the easier it will be for the investor to convert it to cash if the need arises. Even if you do not need the cash, it might be difficult to rebalance your portfolio to its best percentage allocations. However, if you enjoy the aesthetics of fine art and rare items, you might decide it is worth collecting what you like. With prudent selection, you might be able to make a profit. There are not many indices of returns on collectibles, but those that exist generally indicate the return is similar or slightly better than the stock market although with higher fluctuations.

Apart from acquiring the knowledge or retaining an expert to advise you, some general principles apply in selecting which collectibles to invest in. Buy the best thing you can afford, and buy it in the best condition you can afford. Widely available collectibles, such as common gold coins of unexceptional quality, seldom increase in value to any great extent. The best quality examples hold their value and push prices upward.

Whether you have an expert advising you, understand why the item is collectible so you can determine whether that reason will always exist and the value remain. A historical reason the item is special is better. However, an anniversary plate offered on television or in a magazine, even though it is labeled collectible, might never show much increase in value.

If you are buying from a dealer, make sure he or she is reputable and highly regarded in the field. No matter how much you study, you will probably never know as much as the dealer, so you want to be able to depend on his or her knowledge. If you buy from eBay or at auction, you are vulnerable to being scammed possibly with counterfeit items and often with lower quality goods.

One of the collectible investments you might consider is coins. Coins have many different grading levels, and the best to invest in would be MS 64 or MS 65 or better. These numbers represent the coin's quality on a scale known as the Sheldon Scale, which was named after Dr. William Herbert Sheldon. The scale runs from zero to 70 with 70 denoting a perfect coin. Proof coins made especially for collectors will cost even more but will remain in strong demand when less perfect coins are fluctuating with market forces. Good quality coins will always cost much more than the value of the gold or silver contained in them. They will always vary according to the market, but they are more easily traded than works of art and can represent a good collectible investment.

Currencies
Foreign Stock Markets

Chapter 6: The Makings of Asset Allocation

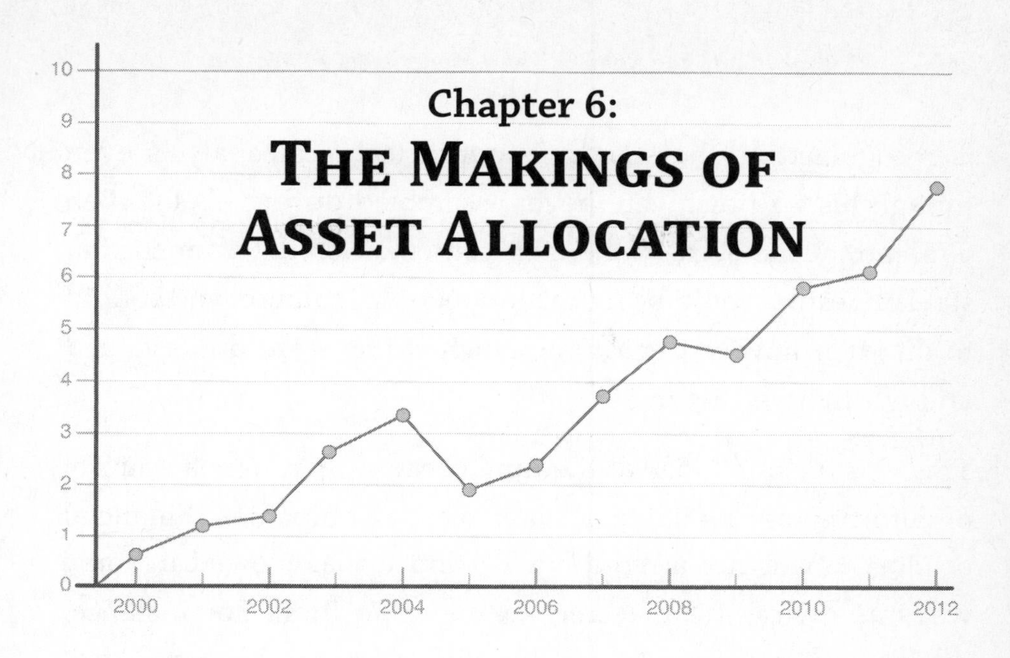

DIVERSIFYING ASSETS TO MANAGE RISK HAS LONG BEEN considered a good idea. About 2,000 years ago, the Talmud said men should always keep their wealth in three forms: one-third in goods, one-third in real estate, and the rest in liquid assets. Bernoulli said in his analysis of the St. Petersburg Paradox in 1738 it was advisable to divide goods that are exposed to danger into several portions rather than risk them altogether. As you can see, the general idea of diversification to reduce risk has been around for as long as people have collected items of value and sought to preserve them.

As far as securities are concerned, Charles Dow famously provided the underpinnings for technical security analysis in his writings in the Wall Street Journal. These were compiled after his death to form what is now known as the Dow Theory, which is recognized as the start of modern technical analysis even though his writings were never assembled during his life. Ben Graham, at the start of the 20th century, was determined that stock investing could be more than mere speculation and sought to discover how to determine which stocks were undervalued and worth investing in.

This was no small task at the time because there was a scarcity of information available on any of the companies. Financial disclosure was not a requirement, and it was viewed in some ways as giving away secrets to the opposition. For instance, during the last decades of the 19th century, the New York Central Railroad issued no reports at all even to its shareholders. Anyone who wanted to analyze the value of a company had to resort to tracking down the information that was available, and sometimes this was found more among personal connections than in published matter.

In some ways, such diligence was ahead of its time. In the 1920s, most people seemed to believe stocks would only increase in value, and they even borrowed money to invest with. This might explain why the collapse in the stock market at the end of 1929 was so dramatic and why it leaves us with those visions of financiers committing suicide in its wake.

Alfred Cowles III, the former heir to and manager of the Chicago Tribune, was one of the thousands of people who the market crash badly affected. This is despite the fact he had exercised due diligence in obtaining substantial written analysis from many of the country's financial analysts, brokerage houses, and insurance companies. The problem was that none of them had given him any warning in advance about the impending stock market crash. It became clear the nation's top financial experts were insufficiently informed to know what was happening in the economy. This lack of foresight caused financial hardships to 90 percent of the country's population.

Diversification

Diversification was thus becoming established as a general strategy to avoid the obvious risks of one security or company failing and wiping out entire savings or investments. However, the emphasis was on individual stock analysis, and despite the stock market crash, there was no immediate connection to any method of dissipating the risk. The best that could be done was to choose stocks and shares that individually seemed to provide some security against loss. Business grew for mutual funds and other portfolio vehicles because they provided a convenient way to package the desired diversification. The first mutual fund launched in the United States in 1924 and was followed by several others. B y 1929, when the market crashed, there were 19 open-end funds with a total of $140 million and nearly 90 closed-end funds holding $3 billion in assets. The diversification offered by these funds meant that investors would have the comfort of knowing their funds were spread across many different financial vehicles, and this was the best to which investors would aspire in those days. Then, diversification was a given. Although, following the stock market crash, many must have wondered how it provided any better investment performance than selecting two or three companies in which to place one's funds.

Cowles and Benjamin Graham, another investor who had faced substantial losses when the stock market crashed, joined with some of the nation's major economists to form the Econometric Society in 1930. The methods employed were better than previously used although not everyone embraced the changes. In 1934, Ben Graham and David Dodd published a book called *Security Analysis* that became required reading for fundamental analysis. Though this book was enlightening for its time, it was only one building block toward the modern idea of asset analysis. It dealt with the way individual stocks could be assessed, and it helped with individual stock picking, but it still did not present a coherent approach to portfolio selection.

Another stepping stone on the path to portfolio theory and asset allocation, John Williams' 1938 book *The Theory of Investment Value* expounded on the value of individual securities and explained how you could determine their intrinsic value with an idea that still is valid today. Williams said stock prices were based on the projected future cash flows discounted to the present day at a suitable rate of interest. In other words, if an investor had a choice between buying the stocks or putting his or her money into a savings account, the returns from the stocks must relate to the interest that would be enjoyed from an investment with a further allowance for the amount of additional risk incurred. As Williams put it, the investment value of a stock is "defined as the present worth of future dividends, or future coupons and principal," and this sets a ceiling on the value of a stock. Williams' idea is called the dividend discount model (DDM).

That this was the first time such mathematics had been applied to determining an investment value is surprising. Williams even apologized in his book's introduction for the fact that he introduced mathematics in deriving stock valuations. But the investing fraternity was in the initial stages of building the framework used today to evaluate equities with such precision. Just as with previous books, Williams did not give specific guidance for an investment portfolio but merely advanced the theoretical aspects. If anything, Williams probably believed any risk on a portfolio could be diversified away. He stated that, "given adequate diversification gains will offset losses. Thus, the net risk turns out to be nil." The term adequate was not defined.

For their part, Graham and Dodd dealt with risk by valuing stocks and bonds and selecting those that, in their view, provided a substantial margin of safety. They looked to buy shares at prices below the company's fundamental net worth, and the cheaper they could buy them at, the better the margin of safety. The idea was if you bought shares with a high expected return at a cheap enough price, the risk would be minimal.

What was lacking was an understanding that an investment portfolio necessarily is greater than the sum of its parts. Graham and Dodd, and later Williams, all looked at securities in isolation. They certainly did their best to provide selection ideas that would pick the stocks with the best chance of performing and growing in value. But simply selecting individual stocks that appear attractive, buying a selection of each, and building a portfolio one security at a time does not address true diversification or interaction.

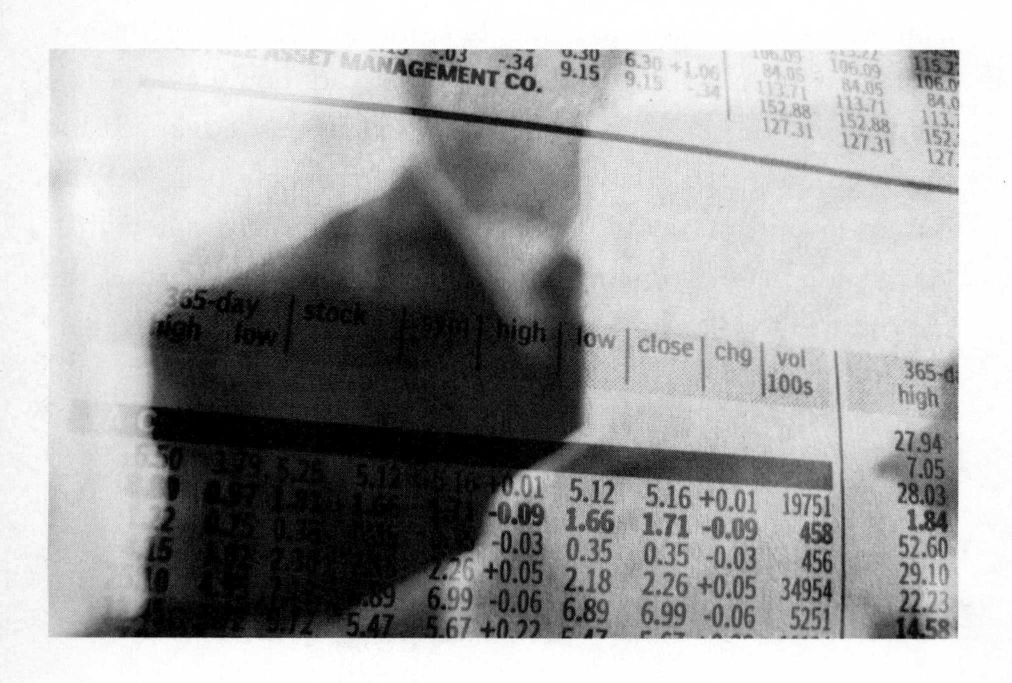

CASE STUDY: ADHERING TO A GAME PLAN

Joseph M. Labella, CIMA®, CAIASM
Director of investments
Diefendorf Capital Planning Associates
Managing director of Consolidated Portfolio Review Corp.
Phone: (516) 759-3900 Ext. 1023
Fax: (516) 759-3928

As a Certified Investment Management Analyst, Joseph M. Labella joins the Diefendorf organization as the managing director of Consolidated Portfolio Review Corp. He earned a bachelor's degree in economics from Fairfield University. Labella spent seven years with Morgan Stanley as a client service representative, portfolio service analyst, and vice president of equity research. He went on to become senior portfolio strategist with UBS Wealth Management for five years. Changing venues, he became an investment consultant for institutional pension, welfare and annuity plans, endowments, and Taft-Hartley funds with Quan-Vest Consultants. His specialty is portfolio construction, and he has published several articles on portfolio construction and equity sector ETFs.

Labella is a life member of the American Association of Individual Investors (AAII) and a member of the board of directors of the NYC Investment Management Consultants Association (IMCA). He is a Chartered Alternative Investment Analyst (CAIA). In addition, he is enrolled in the Certified 3 Dimensional Wealth Practitioner program. Labella has his Series 7, 63, and 65 licenses and received his CIMA® designation in 2004.

Asset allocation is important for individual investors to consider because individual investors, like institutional investors, have varying goals. To achieve these financial goals, individuals must adhere to a game plan. The game plan will be constructed based on the client's risk profile of aggressive, moderate, or conservative; the time horizon; and the asset classes necessary to exceed a target or benchmark return. By using asset allocation, clients can create, monitor, and make changes to the portfolio of investments that will enable them to meet some type of personal or financial goal.

Using an asset allocation strategy offers benefits. Asset allocation, if done properly, will provide the benefits of diversification: lowering the volatility of an individual's portfolio and extracting returns from asset classes that are not widely known or understood. Then, there is the comfort factor, or knowing that although markets will fluctuate, having an asset allocation strategy means the portfolio need not take the same turbulent and costly ride.

Asset allocation and diversification are different. Asset allocation is an actively managed framework, and the diversification benefits are only achieved if the allocation is done properly and is maintained and deliberately adjusted over time. Yes, you can have diversification without asset allocation, but that does not assure a profit or protect against loss in a declining market. The same goes for a poorly constructed asset allocation that fails to provide adequate diversification. A false sense of security develops, and investors are unpleasantly surprised to experience unexpected negative returns when the markets have volatile price moves. To be the most successful, asset allocation and diversification must work together.

When asset allocation appears not to work, the question is not whether asset allocation worked but what was the asset allocation expected to achieve that has disappointed investors in the past. Also, in hindsight, many of the so-called asset allocation strategies were poorly conceived and horribly executed. They failed to consider systemic risk that was not or could not be properly diversified away.

The assumptions made about asset classes and the degree of correlation among several asset classes were not properly vetted during the most recent economic meltdown. In some cases, the asset allocation consisted of only three or four asset classes that began to move in the same downward direction and became one big asset class during the crisis. An old joke about asset allocation is the only thing that moves higher during a market meltdown is correlation. As we saw in the market meltdown in 2008, diversification appeared to be useless.

That diversification isn't working might not be the whole story when returns are severely negative during a period of three to six months. Historical data demonstrates that not all asset classes went down at the same time or to the same degree. Although asset allocation therefore might appear not to function in acute market situations, it does.

Proper tactical asset allocation would have greatly reduced the volatility that occurred in the markets in 2008 and 2009 and would have considerably lessened the loss of wealth.

You should consider several factors that go into making a successful asset allocation strategy. First and foremost is to understand your risk profile. How risk averse or risk seeking are you in the financial construct? And does that risk profile fit with the desired goals you hope to achieve by investing? For example, investing for a child's college education when the child is born is realistic, but trying to invest for the same child one or two years before he or she enters college is unrealistic. The risk parameters and asset allocation at that point are too greatly constrained.

The next factors are the correlation, standard deviation, and expected return of the various asset classes and asset subclasses you wish to use in the asset allocation strategy.

Correlation is the move of one asset class' returns relative to another asset class' returns over time. The goal here is to find various asset classes and subclasses that have a low correlation with each other. A diversified asset allocation strategy helps to reduce the volatility in a portfolio.

Standard deviation is the movement of asset class returns around a central average return, or mean. To which degree away from the average return is the asset class: one, two, or three standard deviations? The greater the standard deviation, the more volatile the entire portfolio will be.

Expected return is the forecast return for each of the various asset classes. When all the returns are calculated on a weighted basis, will the returns be enough to achieve the stated financial goal?

Each of the preceding inputs can be calculated in different ways, and all have weaknesses you need to understood before you allocates any money to a strategy.

We take great strides to ensure all clients, whether individual or institutional, have completed a risk profile questionnaire and have been fully briefed on the riskiness of their investments. The questionnaire assesses the time period, comfort level with investing, and investment knowledge.

We also consider shock analysis, which attempts to visually represent how their investments would have done during several well-known negative market shocks, including the Long Term Capital Management meltdown, the technology bubble, Sept. 11, the wars in Iraq in the early 1990s and in 2003, and the Lehman Brothers collapse.

There is also ongoing monitoring of the client's profile that is addressed on a formal basis annually or sooner if a client's circumstances change.

An ongoing debate in the financial community is whether portfolio rebalancing works and to which degree. Furthermore, the way one rebalances is equal important to successful asset allocation.

Although not exhaustive, the following is a list of the various types of rebalancing:

- **Insured rebalancing:** The portfolio adjusts the allocation of asset classes to a certain predetermined level or a floor value the portfolio should never fall below. It is the equity class that will be affected the most. As equities fall, the portfolio will sell equities to preserve the portfolio. As equities appreciate, the portfolio will allocate more to that asset class. This type of rebalancing explicitly assumes the investors risk profile changes with levels of wealth. Risk below the floor value has zero tolerance, and risk above the floor value has an increased tolerance.

- **Constant mix allocation:** Target weights for each asset class in the portfolio are established based on various capital market assumptions and the client's risk profile. Periodic adjustment restores the portfolio mix as the values of the asset classes change relative to each other.
- **Integrated rebalancing:** This incorporates both a change in capital market assumptions and client risk tolerance and causes an update to target allocation mix. This is the most comprehensive yet timely and resource intensive to implement.
- **Naïve rebalancing:** This is the most common yet least effective because it is purely subjective. Select a date on the calendar and pick a frequency, such as quarterly or yearly, and rebalance back to the initial weights of each asset class. Sell the leaders, and buy the laggards.

First of all, the asset allocation strategies we deploy are only part of our client servicing function. We design an investment policy statement (IPS) with individual and corporate clients. This document, which can vary in length and detail, is paramount for the client to have a successful investment experience and for us to meet the client's expectations. The IPS contains the asset allocation strategy that will be used pursuant to the client's realistic financial goals and their risk tolerance, which we take great pains to ascertain.

Asset allocation cannot hurt an investor's portfolio returns, but it can be perceived as limiting returns. Investors forget the other side of the financial coin is risk, or volatility. To have a successful asset allocation, you want to achieve your goals on the upside but hedge exposure by diversifying if some asset classes start to underperform. In the same vein, investors might be too rigid in their beliefs. If they think they have a well-diversified asset allocation and subscribe to the ill-fated buy and hold strategy, their performance would suffer because they failed to rebalance and incorporate a more tactical approach to their asset allocation before a negative shock occured to their portfolio.

Anecdotally speaking, that your client isn't particularly happy or upset about the asset allocation you constructed for him or her is a sign of a well-constructed asset allocation portfolio.

The efficient frontier is an easy but crude way of mathematically trying to indicate risk and return. The linear assumptions fail to take into account the nonlinear, real world of risk. Furthermore, the optimizers people use to find the optimum mix of assets that sit on the efficient frontier can be misleading when the assumptions used in these factors, including correlation, standard deviation, and expected return, are flawed. As the chart shows, the major tenet of the efficient frontier is that as you take more risk, the potential for return is higher. This tenet was flipped on its head during the time period noted.

By modifying the inputs and placing constraints on the optimizers that go into constructing the efficient frontier, the resulting asset allocation set will be much more robust in its diversification and more applicable to the financial realities confronting the investor.

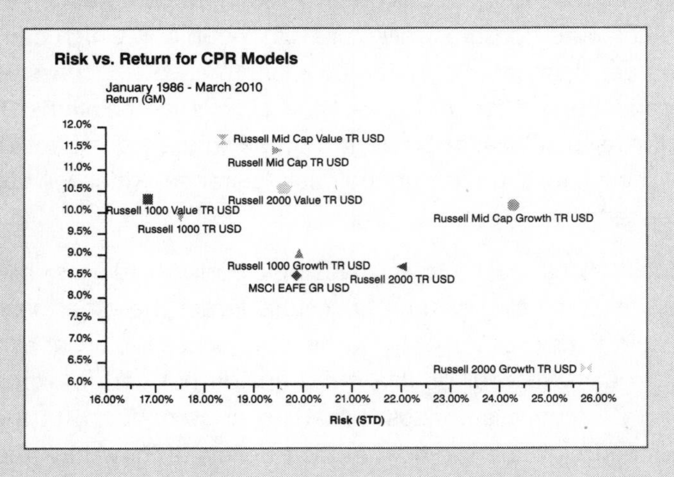

Portfolio Selection

Although the knowledge that diversification was a wise action was common, true understanding of how it might help a portfolio was lacking, and publications generally spoke of the desirability without providing specific reasons. Perhaps the most notable event building up to the current state of asset allocation was the publication in 1952 of a 14-page article called "Portfolio Selection." Harry Markowitz, a 25-year-old student, wrote it, and the *Journal of Finance* magazine published it. It was only with this article diversification of assets became a subject of theoretical study. The article mathematically related risk and return, accepted the need for risk to achieve high returns, and showed how diversification can control risk.

The way Markowitz looked at portfolio selection was in complete contrast to Graham, Dodd, and Williams. Markowitz took a top-down strategy in considering the portfolio and its interactions as a whole whereas the others looked at stock selection as a bottom-up exercise. Markowitz's goal was to explain how to build an efficient portfolio, not how to find individual likely winners.

Despite its importance now, "Portfolio Selection" was hardly recognized when it was published, and academics tended to regard it as too basic. Markowitz expanded on the theory of diversification and quantified how it could work to achieve something close to a desirable portfolio, and this might have been the first time the academic financial world was exposed to a realistic assessment of risk and reward. Markowitz expanded on his theme in a 1959 book titled *Portfolio Selection: Efficient Diversification of Investments*. This work gave him the recognition he deserved, which culminated in a Nobel Prize in 1990.

Markowitz's paper was revolutionary in pointing out the value of security analysis in the context of a whole portfolio rather than breaking it down into individually analyzed parts. The article even suggested that analyzing securities without considering the larger portfolio could be misleading. The security that seems desirable in isolation might be of lesser or even negative importance in a portfolio, and one that does not appear attractive on its own could prove valuable in the context of other stocks.

Markowitz clearly spelled out the mathematical basis and the importance of finding securities that moved independently from each other to reduce the portfolio's risk. The key was simply to find enough securities that exhibited such independence. Although not recognized until later, Markowitz's work on portfolio theory was just as significant as Graham and Dodd's work on fundamentals of securities.

What Markowitz realized and expounded was that by combining securities with little or negative correlation, you achieve real diversification of performance, not the false diversification in which any number of different securities behave similarly and allow a portfolio to suffer despite the variety of stock holdings. By using Markowitz's research and true diversification, building a portfolio that has a lower risk without suffering a lower return is possible.

The reason this is possible is the expected return of a portfolio is a weighted average of the individual expected returns for each security. You must take the average value weighted to account for the different values of securities, and this would be the anticipated gain. On the other hand, the risk is reduced if the relationship between the securities is less than perfect. With a perfect correlation between the securities, the risk remains the same, but a measure of neutrality or of opposite correlation can only lessen the risk. By mixing together securities with the right characteristics, Markowitz showed you can achieve a higher expected return for a given risk, lower the risk for a given return, or develop a combination of these two.

Markowitz also recognized such a portfolio required a carefully selected diversification, and most portfolios that could be made from the general pool of securities would be less efficient than the best because the expected return would be less or the risk would be higher than the optimum. This can be represented graphically on a chart and is now called the efficient frontier, which is illustrated on page 154.

Modern Portfolio Theory

Harry Markowitz was instrumental in exploring and putting forward ways of analyzing investment portfolios. The formal name for his work is the Modern Portfolio Theory (MPT). In his published papers, he explained how to assemble a portfolio by taking proper account of the individual risks and rewards of a variety of investments. Although there have been developments over the years, this theory is still popular with investors who want to avoid taking on too much risk with their money.

The key elements of MPT are as follows:

- By using diversification, investors can lessen the chances of suffering a substantial loss to their account.
- Regular rebalancing of a portfolio to maintain the proportions further controls risk.
- Correlations between asset classes are subject to constant change and movement.

Before the MPT was published, investors made their stock selections by looking at the individual stocks and their expected performance. Each stock would be selected to achieve the best gains with what seemed the least risk. All these selections in one portfolio was thought to be the best investment portfolio you could make. This seemed perfectly logical until Markowitz challenged it.

The challenge was that such a portfolio took no account of any interrelationships or interdependence between the individual investments. For example, transportation stocks seemed to give the best return and least risk, so a portfolio was made up of shares in railroads, air travel, and parcel delivery services. As long as the economy continued on a steady footing, this portfolio might perform well as expected and might be considered diversified to some extent.

But if an energy crisis came about, and the cost of all forms of transportation went up, the performance of the portfolio as a whole could be radically affected. It does not matter that the risk was less for each individual shareholding than investing in manufacturing because the interrelationship between shares means the portfolio was wide open to such a failure.

The advent of MPT called into question this idea of selecting shares in isolation. The key to the theory is to examine the performance of the portfolio as a whole in a realistic way. Though simple diversification into different industry sectors would help avoid a dramatic situation in your account, diversification is no guarantee of a safe portfolio even though it would reduce the risk of loss if one of the asset classes suffered a downturn. Markowitz stated that the risk to individual assets is of less importance than the way all the investments within the portfolio work together. He proposed various mathematical formulas that calculated the combined risk to return ratio of the various asset combinations.

Risk versus Reward

One of the fundamental concepts in investment is that, for a given rate of return, a rational investor will seek the lowest risk investment. Although it is well-understood and almost intuitive that high returns equate to high risk, no relationship for all different types of assets is uniform. It can be assumed a given rate of return has an entire range of risk or a given level of risk has a range of returns. If all other factors are equal, an investor choosing the lowest level of risk for a given return is known as being risk-averse, or avoiding unnecessary risk.

Plotting on a graph the relationship between risk and reward for different investments is possible and often done with the risk increasing from left to right and the return increasing with height. The following is such a chart.

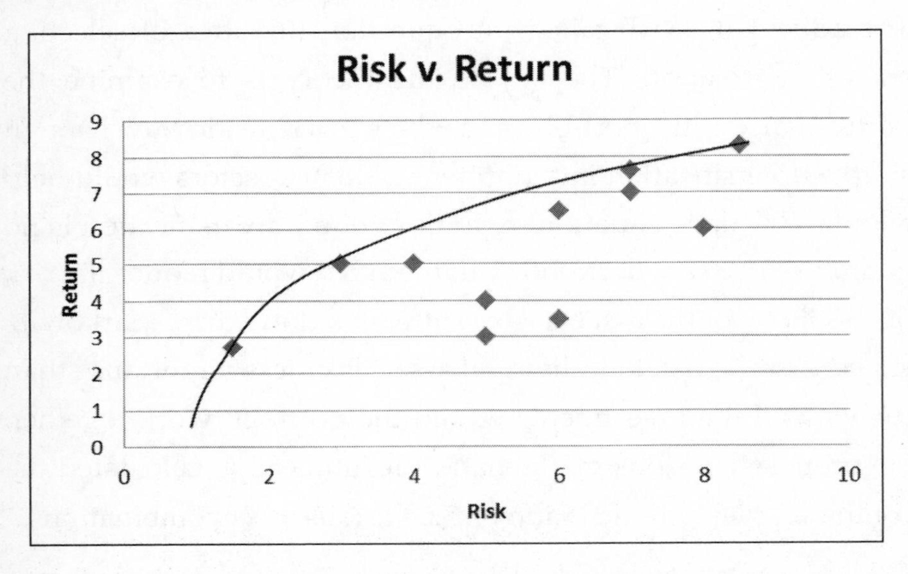

In this graph, out of two points that give a 5 percent return, one has a risk of 3 and the other has a risk of 4. A rational investor would probably choose the lower risk of 3 if all other factors were equal. There are also two points with a risk of 6, one of which gives a 3.5 percent return and the other a 6.5 percent return. The rational investor would choose the higher return for a given risk so would prefer the 6.5 percent.

As you go to the left, the risk reduces, and as you go up, the return increases. A prudent investor would want to go as far to the left and as far up as the asset classes allowed, and the limit of this relationship is shown by the line. No risk-return relationships are available beyond it. You cannot get a return of 5 percent with a risk fewer than 3, and even if you choose a risk of 6, you have no options that exceed 7.5 percent return on this particular chart.

The line drawn, which represents the range of the best investments considered individually, is called the efficient frontier. When you use this charting method to show individual securities, the chart shows you the most advantageous investments for risk versus return. You can also use such a chart to show combinations of securities that make up a portfolio, and this gives you a powerful graphical way to determine the best performance.

The efficient frontier, although simple, is a powerful concept. There is just no point in considering investments that fall a long way to the right or below the line because you know better investments are available. The investments that fall on or close to the line are the most efficient, or best you can get. If a particular investment or combination of investments that lie on the line do not get you the return you need, the only way you can increase the probable return is to take on more risk and move up and to the right along the line. The amount of risk you are prepared to take on will limit your returns. *Chapter 7 discusses this concept in relation to setting up a portfolio.*

Once Markowitz opened the eyes of investors to the possibilities of looking at a portfolio as a whole, other writers furthered the research. James Tobin penned the next critical piece of portfolio theory in 1958. Tobin was an economics professor at Yale, and he started the modern idea of asset allocation.

Tobin had an interesting idea about developing an optimum portfolio. Streamlining the process, Tobin recognized multiple efficient portfolios lie on the efficient frontier, and each has associated risks and returns, which gives investors a choice of how much risk they were prepared to incur for an expected return. Tobin had no time for a host of efficient portfolios with different risk and reward figures. In Tobin's world, it should be possible to find one superefficient portfolio every investor would own. The superefficient portfolio would always be better than any other efficient portfolios.

At first glance, this sounds like a silly proposition. Every investor is different with different risk profiles and different goals. Those who want their money in two years time might select a different set of equities than a recent graduate who is trying to start saving for retirement early. But Tobin was not asserting everyone's portfolio should consist solely of the superefficient portfolio investment.

Tobin's idea was every investor should hold a certain amount of the superefficient portfolio and the rest of their investment should be risk-free assets, such as Treasury bills. By adjusting the proportions of each, every individual investor could select an portfolio to match his or her risk tolerance and generate the greatest possible returns for that selection.

In Tobin's simplified world, only two asset classes should be considered: the superefficient portfolio with some risk and a risk-free asset, such as Treasury bills. Use Markowitz's work to find the superefficient portfolio, and then determine how much of your investment should be in the superefficient portfolio and how much in a risk-free component. The percentages are continuously variable, and with a fervent appetite for risk, the aggressive investor could even borrow money and leverage more than 100 percent into the superefficient portfolio. Both Markowitz and Tobin had opened the door to investors by devising a quantitative way they could design their portfolios.

Although Markowitz and Tobin had tremendously advanced the way portfolio selection might be considered, they were still ahead of their time because the computing power to research these portfolios had not been developed. If the computers were available, there probably wouldn't be sufficient data because such measurement was still in its infancy. The next development was in the 60s when economist William Sharpe advanced portfolio theory with "Capital Asset Prices: A Theory of Market Equilibrium Under Conditions of Risk."

Sharpe built on the work of Markowitz and Tobin by taking what were theoretical positions and turning them into a more practical idea by implementing simplifications. His work became known as the capital asset pricing model (CAPM), and it changed the way people thought about markets.

In the simplified model, owning the market is the same as owning the superefficient portfolio with the highest expected return for a given level of risk. The market is made up of all the world's assets, including stocks, shares, bonds, commodities, real estate, and art. Everything is perfectly priced and tradable.

Once you have accepted the simplifications, some interesting conclusions can flow out of them. For instance, everything exhibits what is called systematic risk, which is simply the market's influence. Other influences are called unsystematic risks. Because systematic risk is unavoidable, it will always exist to some extent in a diversified portfolio. This risk is called beta risk, and it explains why some securities give higher or lower returns than others. A higher return can only come through a higher beta risk. Assets the market does not affect, such as cash, have a beta of zero.

However, unsystematic risk also has an effect on prices. The term coined for this type of risk is alpha, which includes everything that is not beta. Every security has a mix of the two, but alpha can be avoided. The best way is by diversifying your portfolio because the alpha risks will tend to cancel each other. In summary, Sharpe said it is not possible to beat the market, and the best you can do is to own the market and lose only when economic conditions force everything down.

Once again, the theory was ahead of its time. In this case, computer development was not needed. A simple way to buy the whole market so you could implement Sharpe's theory was needed. You would need to buy all stocks in proportion to their market share, which simply was not practical at the time because index funds were not invented until the 1970s, and the first index mutual fund became generally available in 1976. To buy the whole market would require purchasing all the different securities available, and even if you determined to do that, it would be prohibitively expensive because trading commissions were high until after they were deregulated in 1975.

This idea, acceptable now, was hard to swallow in the 1960s when successful money managers were treated like movie stars. Finding active money managers whose strategies seemed to be working was known as chasing alpha. Sharpe's findings asserted that trying to beat the market is misguided, and the educated investor should instead rely on the performance of the whole market portfolio. Although different managers might have better performance from time to time, it is difficult for them to be consistent. Without the practical means to invest in the whole market, Sharpe's theory remained just an interesting hypothesis of no proven or practical value for many years.

The idea that analysts cannot predict future prices with any consistency was not new, however. Around 1900, Louis Bachelier had given a learned dissertation in Paris that was widely ignored at the time. It asserted the French stock and options market had no reasonably recognizable pattern. Bachelier was an advocate of what later became known as the Random Walk Theory, and although it now has its detractors, the dissertation was found later to be of material interest to the researchers and was many years ahead of its time.

The fact that few professional investors beat the market consistently over time tends to support this view, but the truth would seem to be a mixture. In 1965, Eugene Fama wrote in an article titled "The Behavior of Stock-Market Prices" that "the primary concern of the average investor should be portfolio analysis." This led to his recommendations that an investor should decide on a balance of risk and return that was acceptable, review securities for risk factors, and determine how the risks interacted when making a portfolio. In effect, he was advocating asset allocation even before the tools existed with which to quantify the recommendations.

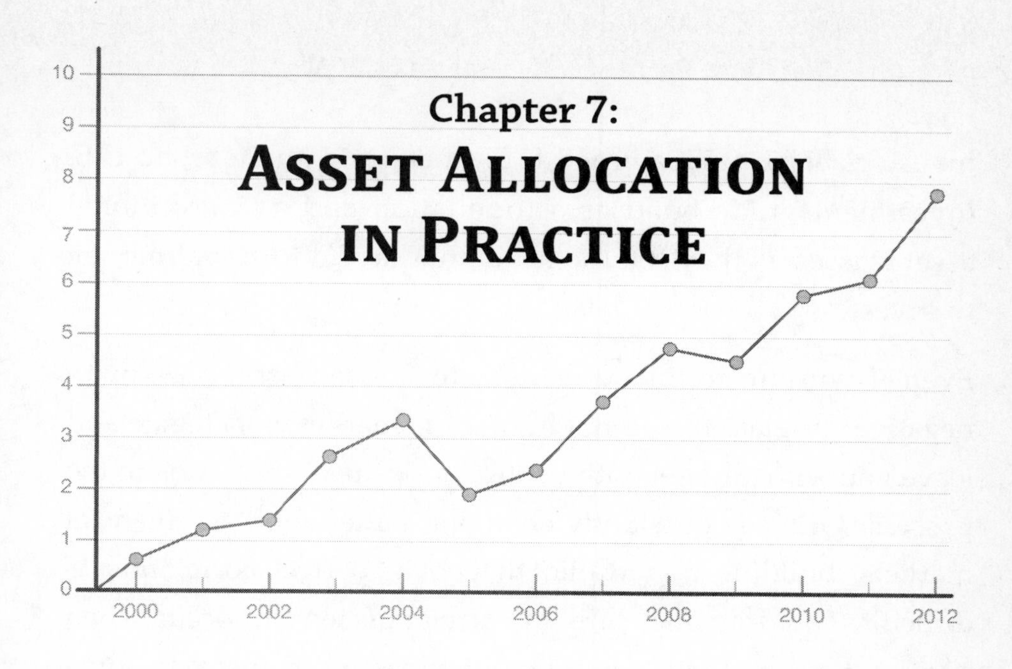

Chapter 7: Asset Allocation in Practice

PREVIOUS CHAPTERS SHOWED HOW MANY different types of investments you can choose from to get the advantages for your portfolio of asset allocation's reduced risk. In principle, asset allocation is a simple process that involves choosing investments that have the highest return with the least amount of risk. If the investor chooses his or her asset classes carefully, has a proper balance of fixed income and equities along with other asset classes if desired, and is diligent in rebalancing the portfolio when required, he or she will have a more successful portfolio.

Principles of Choice

By starting with fixed income and equity mixes, you are able to create a portfolio that has a decent chance of providing you with a good return for the long term. This is why many U.S.

investors begin with a broad U.S. stock fund and a broad U.S. investment grade bond as a foundation and add additional asset classes as they see the need and have additional money to invest.

Even if you are fortunate enough to find an asset class with negative correlation, you might find the market will change and leave you with an asset with neutral or positive correlation in the process. With the constantly changing patterns of the financial markets, building a portfolio that is in perfect correlation is difficult. The dramatic shifts in correlation tend to occur when you least expect them and when you least need them. In some ways, that is more difficult to deal with than finding assets that are negatively correlated in the first place.

Any investments you are considering for inclusion in your portfolio should comply with three important characteristics:

- All the assets in the investment must be different from the other assets in the portfolio.
- The portfolio should contain investments that have experienced periods of negative correlation, noncorrelation, or low positive correlation with the other portfolio investments.
- The investments should be readily available and have good liquidity so they can be traded freely.

Analyzing the fundamentals of any investment to avoid or minimize any overlap in the securities is essential. Overlap can happen with duplication of securities or with similar holdings. In either case, overlap is when two investments hold securities that are basically the same. This causes a problem because they would be highly prone to correlate positively with one another. It might be impossible to avoid all overlap, and some overlap might be desirable for experienced investors who wish to increase their exposure to certain categories and styles. This style of investing should be reserved for those investors who understand the effects overlap can have on their portfolio diversification and have enough knowledge in the market to make portfolio adjustments for the overlap. However, for the novice investor, any type of securities overlap is detrimental to diversification of the portfolio and should be avoided.

When you are looking for an asset class category to include on your investment list, you have to choose a category that is investable. You need to have a selection of low cost marketable securities in the asset class, such as a no-load mutual fund that avoids commission and sales fees on both front and back ends. If you do not pay commission, the entire investment is available to work for your benefit. Even without fees, you still need to check that the mutual funds you are looking at have low expense ratios to maximize your investment. Selecting a fund with high expenses or that charges fees has no intrinsic advantage because this has not shown to guarantee better performance. Having a fund with no redemption fees also means there is no reduction in benefits when you need to buy and sell to rebalance your portfolio.

Ensure the correlation between the asset category class you are considering and the investment fund or instrument is extremely high. After all, if you have worked hard to assemble a portfolio based on the risk and reward figures for an asset class, you need to follow it through with the actual securities or funds with which you populate your selection. Some asset class categories are only available as expensive package products that are suited more for professional investors and corporations than for individual investors. These investments might be in the form of limited partnerships. Among other disadvantages, those partnerships are expensive, are not liquid, have no tax advantages, and lack regulation. Some asset class categories, such as paintings and other art, are not investment instruments. They are investments in the respect that they are worth money to the investor, but they are not instruments the investor is going to trade in the financial market or be able to rebalance easily.

Diversification is the actual practice of distributing your investments over several asset classes to reduce the potential risk. Asset allocation goes a step beyond in using mathematical formulation of strategies that will reduce risk and create a positive goal. Each of the different assets must be evaluated for its risk and return and considered in conjunction with the other assets during various market conditions to construct a portfolio that has a high potential of achieving the desired return while minimizing the risk.

This methodology has now become so commonplace and popular that asset allocation software is available to financial advisors and to individual investors. You might find asset allocation software available on mutual fund and brokerage firm websites, and the advice you read in magazines is often based on MPT research. Though the information available in the public domain is a good start for those learning about asset allocation strategy, serious investors need much more information before they can begin to design a portfolio that is effective and can provide them with the highest return for the lowest possible risk.

One of the biggest challenges an investor has is to find investments that are not correlated or that have a negative correlation. Often, you might have to settle for a slight positive correlation in practice. If the investments move in the same direction at the same time, they have a strong positive correlation, and using the two together in one portfolio is not helpful. A negative correlation means they move in opposite directions, and this reduces the riskiness of the portfolio.

Unfortunately, many investors in the past have made the mistake of selecting mutual funds that seem to offer different growth values and risk but find, sometimes too late, that these mutual funds were based on similar stocks, such as technology and communication. These were especially hard hit at the beginning of the 21st century. If you are determined to invest through mutual funds, you owe it to yourself to go through the information the mutual fund company offers to determine where the majority of their investments lie and make sure similar stocks do not already appear in your portfolio.

Locating asset classes that have low correlations with one another is difficult for investors. A good starting point is looking at past correlations, but you need to go beyond that level of analysis to see how relationships are evolving between the different stocks and asset classes. You cannot rely on past correlation performance to predict future performance even though you need to take that into account in developing your portfolio. The figures change frequently, and although some classes become more correlated with one another, others will tend to move more independently.

Though having a negative correlation to neutralize risk obviously is best, finding asset classes that will maintain a negative correlation for any length of time is difficult and sometimes impossible. An alternative is to find asset classes that are consistently not well-correlated with each other, and there many more that have a low positive correlation in the long term. Assess these factors by looking through comparisons over 10-year periods. For a well-rounded portfolio, an investor will probably include several of these particular types of investments.

Given the variability of correlation, having several investments that are only sparsely related to each other is important. The intention is to have enough difference that some will move in opposite directions to each other and provide the risk reduction desired. This system is by no means infallible. The numbers only represent probabilities, and sometimes these will coincide to work against you. Asset allocation gives no guarantee of eliminating risk, but when properly applied, it will reduce risk's effect on the portfolio as a whole and decrease the potential for suffering a substantial loss across the board.

With this in mind, suffering a loss in your portfolio in a particular year does not mean your asset allocation strategy is faulty. Though you should examine it to make sure it has no obvious errors or weaknesses, you must accept that losses will happen occasionally. There will always be times in the future, just as there have been in the past, when even the most well-developed portfolio will suffer a loss; this is the nature of the investment market. Asset allocation is the key to avoiding substantial losses by assembling a well-designed and diversified portfolio.

Asset allocation stacks the odds in your favor in the same way you do when you can eat right and exercise regularly. You could still die before your neighbor who is a couch potato and smokes and drinks heavily. No one knows exactly when and how much these financial security prices are going to change, but it makes sense for you to put yourself in the best position to profit from the price movements. If you choose investments that are not on the efficient frontier, you will be taking on more risk for a given expected rate of return or decreasing average returns for the level of risk you select.

In the real world, not all investors maintain the most efficient portfolios. Though they might be aware of the recommendations and strategies that can give them the best asset allocation, there might be reasons they choose to make other selections. If these reasons are simply conscientious objections, such as not wishing to invest in tobacco companies, the efficient frontier can be replotted to exclude objectionable companies, and asset allocation will still give the best chance of returns for the companies allowed. Efficient portfolios sometimes are not maintained because the investor does not commit time to rebalancing to the calculated ideal proportions. *See Chapter 9 for more on this topic.*

The efficient frontier gives the investor a tool with which to analyze risk and return on the path to discovering an efficient and worthwhile portfolio, but not all investors take advantage of this tool. For some, it might be they feel they have the skills necessary to make the right decisions without the benefit of any tools. The efficient frontier is important for any investor looking to optimize his or her portfolio. Financial advisors and brokerage firms can help create financial projections that result in efficient portfolios. Being able to see the potential risk and return using efficient frontier methods can help new investors develop the skills to make the best choices. This will help seasoned investors make sure their choices are reasonable ones.

Investor Behavior

The theories of asset allocation set out important principles to adhere to so your portfolio is optimized. Unfortunately, it only works if investors behave rationally and can exercise discipline when looking after their portfolios. Experience shows many of the observed problems with portfolio performance can be traced to irrational behavior. This has been studied since the 1960s and is known as behavioral finance. It aims to explain how psychology influences an investor's decision-making process.

Key concepts affect the success of the investor. Identifying your risk tolerance is crucial so you do not later undermine your investment selections. A risk questionnaire, such as one a financial advisor might give you, is a starting point for finding out your propensity for risk. *A typical risk questionnaire is given in the Appendix*. A financial specialist or a behavioral psychologist would normally interpret the answers. It is also possible to take an asset allocation stress test to get further insight into your tolerance for risk.

Assessing your personal risk tolerance is essential because going beyond the bounds of what you are able to accept guarantees you will seek ways to change your portfolio, which generally will be to your detriment. Determining your risk tolerance entails quantifying the amount of price volatility and investment loss you are willing or able to withstand without changing your behavior. The perfect portfolio for you would cause concern when the market is in a downward spiral, but it would not be volatile enough to make you change your investment strategy. When a portfolio contains too much risk, it causes an investor to change his or her behavior during periods of high volatility and high stress. The end result is the original investment plan on which the portfolio is based is changed on the fly or even totally abandoned. This can cause an investor to suffer significant losses because he or she will effectively be looking for quick returns rather than assets that will provide long-term profits.

Any time an investor changes or abandons an investment plan because of emotional reasons, risk to the portfolio increases, which in turn reduces potential return from that investment. The trigger for this is when the investor loses money, and if an investor has been suffering from the effects of a bad market for some time, he or she does not want to be on the other side of the fence when it traverses and begins to head in an upward direction. If the investor allows that to happen, the strategy becomes one of all risk with no return. Emotional decisions do not always result in the sale of risky investments, but they might be evidenced by an unwillingness to invest any new money at that time or a willingness to delay rebalancing the portfolio until the market direction is clear.

Timing is essential when it comes to creating and maintaining an efficient portfolio, and focusing on timing the short-term market correctly could lead to substantial losses in the long run. It is easy to think you have more skill than you do, become overconfident, convince yourself you can read the markets, and open yourself to making big mistakes in the future. The market sometimes will act to reinforce this overconfidence by working out well on several subsequent occasions, and this creates an even more vulnerable position in which correct prediction becomes viewed as a virtual certainty rather than sheer good luck.

One of the assumptions with asset allocation is investors will act rationally and exercise caution when managing their portfolios, but in practice many are not this disciplined. A general assumption is that investors completely understand the way the markets work and the way the investments relate to each other before they make any decisions about asset allocation. Also assumed is that, once the asset allocation has been done, the investor will take time to rebalance the portfolio at regular intervals so the target risk and return are achieved. In reality, this does not happen. All investors have good intentions, but they are not all completely rational in their decision-making processes, and they do not always exercise discipline in implementing and maintaining their plans. This has been blamed as the main reason most individual investment portfolios do not perform as well as the markets in which they are invested.

According to research, a significant number of deficiencies in personal investment performance are attributable to irrational behavior and error repetition on the part of the investors. Researchers also discovered these investor flaws are consistent, predictable, and widespread. Studies show investment behavior, not financial markets, cause these deficiencies. The few investors who develop a plan for building their portfolios end up abandoning the plan, which in turn causes their portfolio to suffer and not give the returns expected.

This investor behavior occurs during times when the market is depressed and the investor tries something else or when a portion of the market is experiencing substantial gains and the investor abandons his or her plan to chase the high returns. Both of these reactions show the individual investor has not fully understood the theory behind diversification and reallocation or is prepared to override these principles because of emotions.

One of the major mistakes investors make is underestimating market risk. When an investor adds too much risk to his or her portfolio without fully understanding the danger or knowing what could happen in the event of a downturn in the market, he or she runs the risk of succumbing to emotional irrationality when suffering cyclical losses. Whenever investors become anxious about the asset allocation strategies, they have a tendency to be impulsive. Instead of investing in long-term investments, they will abandon their original plans for what they perceive as a safer option: short-term investments with low returns. This kind of destructive behavior can be avoided by learning to recognize the risks to your portfolio that arise from a particular asset allocation strategy and accepting them as part of your plan. Of course, you have to make sure the risk level of the strategy is below your risk tolerance before you put the plan into place for a specific asset allocation strategy.

Behavioral finance attempts to understand how psychology will affect an investor's decision-making process. It is a relatively new science, but already behavioral finance researchers have assembled a checklist of problems new investors encounter:

- Investors place too much emphasis on recent information and too little on long-term projections.
- People tend to be more optimistic about stocks following an increase in price and more pessimistic after a decrease.
- People choose investments that have recently experienced a large increase in performance. More than 80 percent of investors who purchase mutual funds have bought those with the best return over a one-year period.
- An investor views an investment that has performed well relative to what he or she paid for the asset as good. He or she does not look at the fundamentals of the investment.
- People do not like to admit they are wrong, which explains why they are happy to pay high commissions to brokers and advisers. If the investment turns out badly, they have someone else to blame for the problem.
- In general, investors have too much confidence in the future earning capacity of expensive companies and have too little confidence in the earning capacity of inexpensive companies.

- Some investors, in the belief they are more knowledgeable than they are, tend to overtrade. This almost inevitably leads to excessive commissions and underperformance in the market.
- Most overconfident investors are well-educated men.
- Women have a tendency to invest for the longer-term in the markets more than men do, so their portfolios tend to perform better.

Strategies

When it comes to setting up your investments, you must be more focused on your own particular circumstances and what you are saving for than the general techniques and theories to optimize your portfolio. For many people, the chief purpose of their savings, particularly in later life, is to provide well for their retirement. Other younger investors might have more immediate goals in mind, such as being able to meet college fees for their children. But until you sit down and chart out your requirements, knowing whether you have a reasonable chance to meet your needs in the time available and with the money that you can invest is impossible.

Your investment strategy must be focused on your personal circumstances and what you hope to achieve. Every investor would ask that their money yield the highest possible return with the lowest possible risk, but there could be a need to compromise between risk and return. If you start with some concrete figures, you will have a much better chance of getting to where you want to be.

Start with an accurate assessment of where you stand at present. If you do not currently keep accounts of all your spending, you might have to work from credit card and bank statements to see how much you realistically need to live on. In this case, past history is a good indication of future performance because unless you make a conscious effort to change your habits, your spending will tend to be the same from year to year.

Take into account your current net worth, which includes any equity in your home and vehicles. Against this, you must offset any liabilities such as credit card bills and your mortgage. If you already have substantial savings, this amount will count toward your net worth.

Finally, you need to determine what you think your income is going to be for the coming years. This might be the easiest for you to define if you are in long-term employment and expect to stay at the same or a similar job during your career. If you have rental properties, the income from these would also count in this section although you have offsetting expenses, such as repairs and taxes.

Once you have a good idea of all respects of your financial position, you can proceed in several ways to figure out what your future needs are and how much return on your investments you need to make to achieve them. Figure this out with a pencil and a piece of paper preferably when your affairs are not complicated and you are trying to get a quick estimate.

Another way to approach the summary of your financial life is to prepare a spreadsheet. If you are comfortable using Microsoft Excel, this is the most flexible approach because it allows you to make changes to all the numbers and run different scenarios, for example, changing your career path. An alternative that might be more user-friendly is Quicken or another financial software that will lead you through setting up the accounts and assets and can even keep track of the performance of your investments automatically.

If you think the amount of information you need could overwhelm you or feel you need expert advice, you might engage a financial professional to collate information and do the projections for you. However, even when you use a professional, you need to put your hands on all the information so you will still be involved in a certain amount of work.

When you finally produce the financial projection from this exercise, bear in mind it is not hard and fast, and if your circumstances change, you should go back and modify the amounts appropriately to see the effect.

You might overlook some items. For example, if you have children, you might have to pay for college and wedding expenses when they grow up. Any regular expenses you have need to be adjusted for inflation each year, so your financial needs will grow commensurately. If you are currently at work and saving for retirement, you should try to avoid using any of the common guidelines for what you need as an annual income after retirement. Many variables depend on what you envision doing, and taking a simple percentage, such as 70 percent of your current income level, might not allow for what you foresee in the future.

For example, some people plan to travel when retired to see all the places they had no time to visit when they had a full-time job, and travel can be expensive. On the other hand, the costs of commuting to work, whether by car or train, will go away. It is up to you to be as realistic as you can in assessing what your needs will be and how far any 401(k) plans or Social Security payments will go toward meeting them.

When you have done this work, you will have a much better idea of what you need to do to achieve your goals and whether the goals are practical given your level of income and lifestyle. You can then consider the effects of different levels of risk on your ability to meet your requirements and decide on an acceptable risk level you can live with. If, as with many people, you cannot achieve your goals by investing conservatively, it is up to you to decide whether to accept a high enough risk or moderate your ambitions. It is not worth your while to invest in a portfolio that will keep you awake at night if you have other choices based on a reduction in your desires.

Style of Asset Allocation

After making a thorough assessment of your current financial situation and your projected needs, it is time to work on determining your asset mix. Assembling your portfolio is more than just choosing the assets you want to include. How to mix the assets to create the most profitable combination is essential to understand. Correlation between investments, or the relationship of each asset class to another, is one of the fundamental components in determining the right asset mix for your circumstances.

As the investor, aim for perfect negative correlation in your asset mix. This is impossible to achieve in the real world but theoretically would result in one asset going up when another asset went down at precisely the same time. The next best solution is to create a portfolio with an asset mix as close to ideal as possible to optimize the performance of your portfolio. Optimization in these terms is not necessarily maximizing the return from your portfolio. It includes taking into account the performance risk to achieve good returns with less chance of losses.

While determining how much of each individual asset class to include in your portfolio, take a holistic view of the portfolio. How each individual asset performs in isolation is irrelevant. What is important is how its behavior and characteristics can work harmoniously with other assets as part of the entire portfolio. Whenever you consider adding a particular asset to your portfolio, review the current selection and see how that asset can fit in and improve the performance. A proper asset mix will allow you to take advantage of market fluctuations, not fear them.

The style of an asset allocation can be defined in one of three ways: conservative, moderate, or aggressive. The meaning of these styles can vary depending on the strength of volatility of the market at any given time. A portfolio that is considered moderate when the financial market is stable could be redefined as highly aggressive when the markets exhibit a substantial amount of volatility. This most frequently happens during periods of high inflation when bond prices and interest rates are both suffering considerable fluctuations. During the beginning of the 21st century, asset allocation styles could be considered in these groups:

- **Conservative:** Lower levels of exposure within the equity and equitylike investment markets coupled with higher exposure to cash, short-term investments, fixed income securities, domestic market investments, and currencies. The conservative style of asset allocation will show lower price fluctuations and provide more income in the form of dividends and interest instead of capital gains.
- **Aggressive:** Higher exposure to equities, equitylike investments, and investments in the foreign market. Aggressively styled allocations generally have a lower exposure to cash and short-term investments, fixed income securities, and domestic investments. Aggressive investors

will see more of their profits resulting from capital gains from price volatility and less income from dividends and interest.

- **Moderate:** The moderate style of asset allocation is simply a compromise between the performance of the conservative style and the aggressive style, and investment strategies would fall between these two.

Besides considering the aggressiveness of the style of asset allocation, you can also look at the orientation of the investments. Asset allocation orientation can be defined as either strategic, tactical, or a combination of the two. Strategic asset orientation will focus on the best mix of assets over the long term without undue consideration of the fluctuations that predominate the short-term markets. In this type of asset allocation, the focus is on the following:

- The investor's perspective on financial markets for the present and how this is relevant and relates to the investor's long-term goals.
- The investor's perspective on the long-term goals for any assets that have the potential to create changes within the asset allocation model.
- The investor's means to monitor and to manage any perceived long-term risks that could occur in any of the chosen asset classes.

An investor might choose to use strategic asset allocation for several reasons. One of the more important functions is to determine which investments should be included in the long-term mixture of assets. This can be determined based on the asset class and might also include considering the asset subgroups and their risk exposure over the long term. Some of the classes to which this relates include:

- Small-cap equities
- Emerging market equities
- Convertible securities
- Real estate investment trusts (REITs)

An investor who uses a strategic asset allocation will not often make changes. This type of allocation is used when setting up an account that will not be monitored frequently and is not required for a long time. On the rare occasions a change is made to the strategic asset allocation, it is because of one of the following situations:

- There have been important changes in the investor's life, including the amount of risk to be taken, the expectation of returns from the investments, and future planned events.
- The investor has decided to review and change the acceptable standards of deviations or correlations.
- A new class of assets is introduced to the market that could improve the portfolio, or the investor becomes aware of assets that were previously unknown to him or her.

Expressing the idea of the strategic asset allocation in the form of an investment description or statements the investor writes or a financial advisor writes and the investor adopts can be illuminating. The statement will include the following specifics:

- Return goals
- Risk tolerance
- Preferences and exclusions regarding asset classes
- Ranges and targets for asset allocation strategies
- Time horizon
- Procedures for review of the portfolio for possible rebalancing
- Arrangements for custody and reporting
- Choices and instructions for an investment manager
- Fees and expenses related to the investor's portfolio

These specifics can also act as guidelines for decisions relevant to tactical asset allocation and give a reference for reviewing the conditions of the current financial markets.

Strategic asset allocation can be a helpful tool when extreme volatility in the market causes investors to rethink their decisions about asset allocation. Though these dramatic changes in the financial market can make buying or selling more attractive at any given moment, approaching these changes from a tactical standpoint is more financially feasible than changing the entire strategy because of some short-term fluctuations in the market. The strategic asset allocation can help an investor make important decisions about asset deployment in a disciplined and methodical way.

In contrast, tactical asset allocation is the process of putting into motion the actions that have been determined. Tactical asset allocation involves investors following all of the original plans for their portfolios on a frequent basis. This means dealing with such issues as:

- Carrying out all the practical details of portfolio structuring and choosing or rejecting certain investments.
- Managing the technical aspects of the portfolio, such as purchasing, selling, analyzing, evaluating, monitoring, and measuring the profitability, volatility, and correlations within specific investments.
- Providing instructions for carrying out all portfolio changes.
- Making decisions about suitable and unsuitable investment activities for the portfolio.

Investors who implement tactical asset allocation are seeking results that are superior to those they expect to obtain with strategic allocation alone. Proper implementation of tactical asset allocation will provide investors with a better risk-adjusted return than they would realize with strategic asset allocation. Though strategic asset allocation is the starting point for all portfolios, introducing tactical allocation should improve returns.

Sometimes, there is a case for practicing risk avoidance. Unlike risk tolerance, which an investor would normally wish to adhere to simply because of the emotional pressures that could influence investing if the tolerance level were exceeded, risk avoidance simply means avoiding excessive risk if there is no reason to take it on. In other words, the investor decides he or she will not invest in the market, and his or her portfolio therefore will not reach the risk tolerance level. An investor might choose not to maintain a risky portfolio for many good reasons, and every new investor should understand the need to sometimes exercise risk avoidance instead of retaining risky assets that take your portfolio right up to your risk tolerance.

All portfolios inherently involve some degree of risk, and avoiding the risk completely is impossible if you are in the market. Risk avoidance is a conscious decision to select a portfolio with minimal risk. Although taking risks is necessary to ensure returns, taking on a portfolio that corresponds to the investor's maximum risk tolerance level is not always necessary.

Though an investor with significant financial goals might choose to hold investments at his or her risk tolerance level, another investor who has enough assets in his or her portfolio to sustain a steady cash flow for the rest of his or her life might not need to invest to the peak tolerance level. Maintaining a portfolio with a high level of risk when it is unnecessary can have a negative effect. If a portfolio can give you relatively safe returns at an adequate level, taking on additional risk and the possibility of larger fluctuations even when the risk is within your tolerance level can lead to stress and discomfort.

It is also possible to become too conservative and practice a scheme of risk avoidance that avoids any kind of significant risk, which consequently limits the return potential. There is no need to try to eliminate all risk from a portfolio even if you have enough invested to meet your financial goals. There will always be a certain amount of risk in any portfolio no matter how well the market might be doing at any given time. With correct asset selection, each asset class moves somewhat independently from the rest of the portfolio, so it is likely some of the assets will be increasing even while others are decreasing because of market fluctuations and volatility.

All investments, no matter how carefully planned, have some risk involved because they will face the effects of both inflation and taxes. Choosing to retain some assets with a higher risk factor in the portfolio has the advantage of providing an additional return after taxes. Even if the investor does not need this for living expenses, it will give an extra boost to the assets left behind as an inheritance. This supplies a welcome income for the investor's heirs and provides a future for those an investor might leave behind.

Choosing to maintain a risk level below the portfolio's maximum risk tolerance is a decision each investor needs to make for him or herself, and it should be made without regard to predictions on the stock market or the ideas of financial experts. When you choose to reduce risk at the appropriate time, you will not lose the built-in financial security even if the market goes on a downward spiral without warning.

Although asset allocation, asset diversification, and rebalancing are all key to managing a portfolio, there might be times when even these elements fail and the portfolio suffers a loss. This does not mean the portfolio has been incorrectly constructed. These situations just occur because it is impossible to predict the market all the time. An experienced investor learns how to structure the portfolio to be exposed to the least amount of risk in the event the market starts to plummet. The market has seen a great many downturns over the years, and this will likely continue into the future. However, the smart investor will manage his or her portfolio to be able to tolerate the occasional loss while still retaining financial security and providing healthy returns.

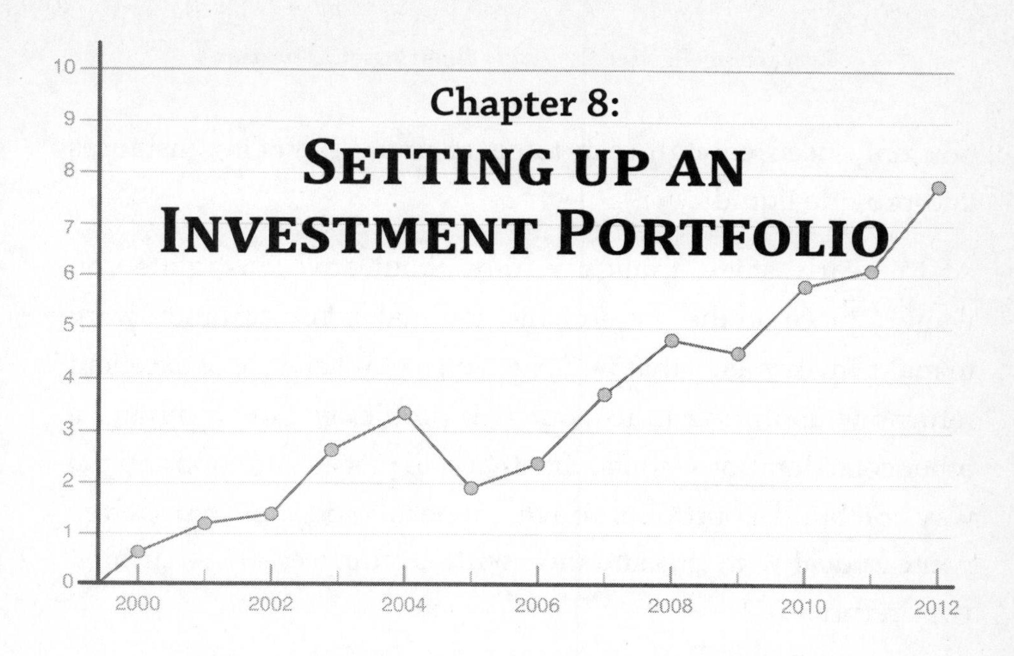

Chapter 8:
Setting up an Investment Portfolio

BUILDING AN INVESTMENT PORTFOLIO GOES FAR BEYOND simply buying securities and other investments. As you can see from the previous chapter, there is a lot of homework to be done before you are ready to select the securities that will make up your portfolio. You can purchase securities in several ways.

Bearing in mind your risk tolerance, determine the proportions of the different types of financial instruments you wish to include in your account. Some types of assets belong in every account while others' inclusion might depend on your personal preferences. For instance, to keep up with and beat inflation, even the most conservative portfolio should include some equities and stocks. These might not be the same equities you would include in an aggressive portfolio, however. Cash and cash equivalents can also be useful but are the least successful at keeping up with inflation.

You only need enough cash to cover unforeseen circumstances and provide liquidity.

At this early stage, think carefully about any constraints you want to place on the investments you make. You certainly want to make investments that will give you a good chance of excellent returns while fitting in to your risk profile, but there might be other considerations to evaluate that will place restrictions on the way you build a portfolio. You might need to do some research so you can deal with this situation without unnecessarily harming your returns.

Limiting Factors

Three factors could possibly affect your investment strategy and deter you from creating a portfolio strictly in accordance with the numbers. These factors include having investments you do not want to part with, not placing investments with companies you would never consider, and restricting your investments to some others.

There might be some assets in your portfolio with which you refuse to part for emotional reasons. For instance, you might have stocks that are inherited from a deceased family member, and you want to hold onto them for sentimental reasons. You might have invested in your best friend's start-up company and are determined to stand by that investment regardless of performance.

There can be other reasons for holding onto stock regardless of whether it is making a profit. You might own shares of your employer's stock and be under a legal constraint not to sell it for a specific period of time. Generally, the advice would be not to invest too heavily in the company that is also responsible for your paycheck because any problems with the company might affect your job and your portfolio. But conditions are attached to buying or receiving company shares, and these commonly include not turning around and selling them right away. The strategy for building and rebalancing your portfolio is largely the same with these investments as with any others you will not part with; you need to work around any perceived limitations in diversity or other factors and include them as part of your portfolio.

Another class of investments might affect the way you develop your portfolio: investments you would never consider regardless of how well they would otherwise fit in with your portfolio. You might decide you do not want to invest money in a particular company for several reasons. For instance, many people think twice before investing in a tobacco company, and your feelings might be particularly strong if you believe smoking tobacco has was a factor in the death of a family member or close friend.

There might also be restrictions on investing in companies for which you are privy to insider information, such as ones your company consults or audits. Even if you do not have specific insider information, many people feel they must avoid any appearance of a conflict to avoid accusations in the case the shares perform exceptionally well. With 8,000 companies on the U.S. stock exchange, there is simply no reason you need to invest in one that could cause problems for you later. Similar reasoning would apply to investing in your company's competitors. Even though you would not have access to insider information, you could be embarrassed by this action if it became known.

As with the companies you would not part with, you can work around any perceived limitations by selecting equivalent investments about which you have no reservations. The strategy for building and rebalancing your portfolio excluding the investments you dislike is to work around the restrictions and select viable alternatives.

The third class of company is that which you have reservations about investing in but do not want to exclude totally from your portfolio, particularly if doing so might involve effectively eliminating complete industries from your investments. Such companies might include health care facilities that perform abortions or companies promoting gambling. By necessity, you would have to wrestle with your conscience about the extent to which you could be involved with companies you believe might have some laudable aspects but also promote practices with which you disagree.

CASE STUDY: DISPERSING YOUR RISK

Mark Kennedy
Kennedy Wealth Management LLC /
Kennedy Financial & Insurance Services Inc.
21550 Oxnard Street, 3rd Floor
Woodland Hills, CA 91367
Phone: Toll Free: 888-805-1541 Local: 818-224-6074
Fax: 818-224-6073
markk@markkennedyonline.com

Mark Kennedy, the president and founder of Kennedy Financial & Insurance Services Inc. and Kennedy Wealth Management LLC, and a registered investment advisor, has proudly helped more than 1,200 individuals and families with their wealth planning needs for more than a decade. Kennedy is a specialist in the Retiree Wealth Transfer/Preservation Market and also in the Small Business Pension Planning Market. Both firms are located in Woodland Hills, California.

Asset allocation is important for individual investors to consider because with today's volatile investing environment, risk needs to be spread out among different asset classes. Asset allocation within different sectors of stocks, for instance, is not enough today. Investors need to consider alternate asset classes beyond stocks, such as commodities, currencies, and hedged equity, or short positions. An individual investor should not go it alone. He or she should consider a professional money manager whose team has extensive knowledge and experience with trading these alternative asset classes.

The benefits of using an asset allocation strategy are that the individual investor can minimize exposure derived from a single market, such as the stock market, and obtain a gain when the equity market is losing ground. For example, a currency piece of the asset allocation strategy could help an investor stabilize or even make money when the equity markets are going down. Diversification, according to many of the major brokerage firms, is buying into different sectors of the stock market, such as technology, raw materials, manufacturing, and health care, with the intention these sectors are negatively correlated. When one sector goes down, the other rises. Diversification can go further by using international stocks and diversifying within their given sectors. Asset allocation is true diversification. However, to achieve asset allocation, you cannot stay in just one market, for example, the U.S. stock market, and expect this to be enough to minimize risk and maximize gain. Today, the individual investor should think like the institutions and invest in a broad range of investment types. Commodities, currencies, and hedged equities are a few.

Asset allocation might not work, for example, investing in the same type of market even though the investor might be in small-cap and large-cap stocks. This is not true asset allocation. However, most brokerages would make an investor think so.

When using an asset allocation strategy, investors must consider their comfort with low, medium or high risk. Not all asset classes are right for certain types of investors. For example, commodities and currencies can be considered higher in risk; however, these can see less drawdown on a market decline than typical equities when properly managed by an experienced management team. So, the management team is imperative.

We use an Investor DNA risk tolerance questionnaire to gauge the investing style and risk tolerance of the client. This consists of several dozen questions about their psychological investing behavior. We hand the results over to a professional management team that uses a sophisticated analysis on the questionnaire. This step is imperative to designing a portfolio with asset classes that match the investor's risk.

In my view, rebalancing does not always work. You could be rebalancing out of asset classes that are going up in value and rebalancing into asset classes that are losing value.

We have a professional outside management team that specializes in "alternative" investment classes, such as commodities, real estate, currencies, and short equity positions. The team positions clients depending on the amount of assets being managed, their goals, and their risk tolerance.

Incorrect asset allocation can hurt an investor's returns. You would not want to put a client into a positively or closely correlated portfolio. For example, you would not want to put an entire client's portfolio within small-cap stocks and large-cap stocks and then say the he or she was asset allocated. Some advisors and firms would call that asset allocation. I would not.

I believe the efficient frontier is an accurate indicator of investor expectations relative to risk versus returns.

Long-term Goals

When you start to put together the percentages of different assets you want to include in your portfolio, bear in mind these should be selected for the long term. *Chapter 9 looks at rebalancing your portfolio to restore the original asset allocation percentages*. This is the usual maintenance exercise you will perform at regular intervals. Unless your circumstances change or there is a shift in the performance of the markets, you will not tamper with the established percentages of the asset classes.

The assets in your portfolio might be held in different accounts but should be considered as a whole. Sometimes holding particular asset classes in a certain way, such as in a self-directed IRA, is more tax efficient. *This will be discussed in more detail in Chapter 10.*

Never lose sight of the total mix because this is what represents your actual wealth, and if you have a 401(k) scheme at work, you might be restricted to a number of funds that only represent part of the asset classes you want to include. An active 401(k) account should grow all the time from continued contributions and capital gains, so this might require you to undertake your rebalancing exercise more frequently.

When you consider your asset class percentage allocations, realize that the optimal percentages might be impossible to determine. Only in retrospect can you see how the various asset classes have performed, and if the characteristics of the financial securities have varied from the historical values you based your selection on, the allocation will have been less than perfect. As long as you are considering your needs and your propensity for risk when setting the percentages, the fact you have even come this far in controlling your portfolio means you are better off than many other investors. You certainly should not consider refining the percentages to better than the nearest 5 percent, and that degree of accuracy will be perfectly adequate to give you good performance.

Formal analysis of the optimal allocation percentages is taken care of with software when you visit a financial advisor. The software includes the expected total return for the asset class together with the volatility that can be anticipated, which translates into the risk to the investment. Importantly, the software has been preprogrammed with the exact correlation figures between all the different types of asset classes being considered.

Though professional asset allocation software can be expensive, the Internet offers a number of free or inexpensive options. Use them at your own risk because the performance of these generally cannot be guaranteed, but some programs give a large amount of information that can start you on the right path. You will also find you can obtain demo versions of the more expensive programs so you can assess whether they would be useful to you.

Whether you choose to obtain your own software or decide to use a professional financial analyst to set you on the right track, you will come up with general asset class percentages you want to consider for your portfolio. Setting up an Excel spreadsheet into which you can plug the average returns for the different asset classes and determine the effect different percentages have on your capital growth over the years is a simple matter.

Software programs that make it easy for you to make informed decisions about asset allocation are based on a quantitative approach to identifying the classes and securities. You will go through several steps in determining your optimal asset allocation.

The first step is to select asset classes and subclasses. The use of software makes this much easier, but the principle is the same whether you are using financial data or a computer program.

You want to choose those investments that have previously been profitable and look as though they are continuing in this way. Past performance is no guarantee of future results, but a strong trend will tend to continue, and you can see signs when trends start to slow. At this stage, you want to check that the classes and subclasses that you are considering have negative, zero, or little correlation to one another and the risk is within your risk tolerance.

Now, you can research your shortlist of securities by looking at past investment performance, standard deviations, and the way the returns correlated over different time frames, which might range from a couple of years to as many as 30 or 40. You can review the risk factors of the possible investments and compare these using the standard deviations and look at the expectations of future returns.

As a third step, you need to implement a portfolio optimization program. This will look at each asset class and assign risk and return projections. Based on the results of this analysis, sample portfolios can be assembled and plotted to find those that are on the efficient frontier. A range of portfolios will be available. Each will have minimal risk for the projected return expectation.

Because all the investments along the efficient frontier line are equally efficient, the only way to increase the portfolio return is to increase the amount of risk incurred. It is not necessary to take on your maximum level of tolerable risk if you find you can achieve the returns you need at a lesser level. Though many people would try for the maximum return available, the reduction in risk and the peace of mind in settling for a lower risk level when the expected returns are sufficient for your needs can give you more acceptable choice.

If you are using software, you can set up your own higher and lower percentage limits for the maximum and minimum acceptable amounts in the portfolio. In this final step, you are placing constraints on the optimization software. However good you think the portfolio optimization software is, it is wise to view with a critical eye the output the software produces, not depend solely on it. Because computer programs only process information such as return, risk, and correlation projections, they cannot always take into account the previous history of the assets.

A manual review of the price history will show what the historical values have been for those assets and keep you from choosing investments that could create substantial losses. The purpose of this portfolio optimization is to help investors choose those assets that will allow them to remain within their risk tolerance level and provide them with the highest level of returns. Another reason to review the results manually is to check whether they are consistent with your requirements because computerized portfolio optimization programs often do not allow for the adjustments necessary for high transaction costs and taxes.

You can also use a qualitative approach to constructing the portfolio, and it will work with the quantitative tools. It can also provide the primary input for designing the portfolio. The elements of the qualitative asset allocation frequently depend on various types of historical data, such as charts, statistical tools, and other essential models of data collection. The chief difference between the qualitative and quantitative approaches to asset allocation is the quantitative approach relies on mathematical formulas and computer software programs that basically calculate all possible scenarios while the qualitative approach is contingent upon human judgment.

The qualitative approach to asset allocation looks at several different types of methodology during its assessment process. The measures that might be considered during the qualitative asset allocation process include:

- Fundamental measures, which include various economic indicators; earnings estimates and reports; and other monitoring conditions, such as changes in salaries, prices, and productivity.
- Valuation measures, which takes into account real interest rates and P/E ratios.
- Psychology, technical, and liquidity measures, which include the flow of funds, investor sentiment indicators, volatility indexes, and technical charts.

Another important part of the qualitative approach is the way information is developed for the long term. The methodology involves the investor consulting with experts about assumptions, previous returns, and projections for future and includes cross-asset relativity to develop a feel for the financial feasibility of each investment. Reflection, common sense and the ability to think rationally are necessary in the selection and development of qualitative and quantitative methods of asset allocation. None of the available tools for development of allocation packages would be useful if the investor could not leverage these tools with some intellectual knowledge of his or her own.

For the long-term investor, purchasing power risk, or the risk of loss in cash value due to inflation, is a real and important concern. It can be just as important as the market price volatility risk that might occur over several time periods. On the other hand, short-term investors might find market price volatility of much greater importance than the risk of their assets losing value because of inflation. This mainly is due to the fact they do not have the opportunity to offset good and bad years against one another in the same way long-term investors can. These concerns over time lead investors to place greater emphasis on some essential factors:

- For long-term portfolios, the emphasis is on equity and equitylike assets that have a higher volatility but also exhibit higher returns over the long term.
- For short-term portfolios, the emphasis is on assets that generate interest but have lower long-term returns and volatility.

Investors who require specific income from their investments and are looking to create a long-term investment portfolio might wish to meet the income requirement in one of two ways:

- Spend minimal amounts of cash from the body of the portfolio or from capital gains to increase the income from dividends and interest.
- Create a portfolio that can meet the investor's predefined income requirements solely from dividends and interest payments.

Investors who use the latter method do so because they believe placing too much emphasis on assets that can help them generate substantial income from dividends and interest payments will prevent the generation of other income sources. They feel this limitation might cause them to lose the opportunity to generate significant capital growth from equities and equitylike assets. Each investor should base a decision about the right method for asset allocation on several different factors, including:

- The level of risk he or she is willing or able to assume
- The investment's duration: short-term or long-term
- Income expectations
- Amount of cash available for investment

All these factors have a significant bearing on the type of asset allocation an investor should consider. Those investors with substantial accumulated wealth might need to have more than one type of asset allocation or even more than one portfolio. The key factor is to use the method that will allow the highest level of income with the least amount of risk, and that will vary with each investor.

To give you an idea of the sort of results you should expect when you have gone through the whole process, here are some guidelines of the percentages you should be looking at for each type of asset allocation. Your fixed income portion will be highest for conservative investors and might be anything between 35 percent and 60 percent. A moderate investor would see between 15 and 35 percent of the relatively safe fixed income assets whereas an aggressive investor would choose to have less than 15 percent in this class of asset.

Turning now to equities and stocks, which constitute the highest potential return but also the most risk, a general rule for the conservative investor is to have between 15 percent and a maximum of 40 percent invested in such financial securities. A moderate investor, by definition prepared to take a little more risk, would have between 40 and 65 percent in shares, and the aggressive investor would have more than 60 percent.

Although the portfolio could be made up of just these two asset classes, you normally would include other classes for diversification. For other features, such as their independence from the others, this is their lack of correlation. You might have some real estate or other alternative investments that would constitute one-quarter of your portfolio's value. If doing the sums with correlations, you might want to increase or decrease this proportion by 10 percent, but it is worthwhile to have at least 15 percent of your portfolio in something other than stocks and bonds.

The percentages given above are in ranges for two reasons. First, the division between aggressive, moderate, and conservative investors is not clear-cut. If you are a slightly aggressive investor, you will not want as great of a percentage of equities as an aggressive investor, but you might want more than a moderate investor. You can choose on a sliding scale exactly which level of risk suits you. Second, markets go through cycles, and during turbulent times of high inflation, you might find the same investments considered to be more aggressive. By giving a range of percentages, you can take into account the current market conditions.

Security Selection

When deciding on the proportion of the various asset classes you want in your portfolio, you will work with the generally accepted and historically established figures for those asset class returns and risks. The next step will be to start selecting securities you wish to include in your portfolio. As you select the specific securities, you must assign them to the various asset classes you are considering and make sure the selected percentages are achieved. The other part of this exercise is to determine which accounts will hold which securities. Although it might not seem important to have different investment accounts for different securities, you need to allow for other factors, such as the tax situation and even protection from lawsuits, when deciding the best place to hold investments.

Though your initial goals are important, you have to continue monitoring your portfolio to be a successful investor. Monitoring your portfolio is essential because it shows you when it is necessary to rebalance. *Rebalancing will be described in Chapter 9.* You also need to monitor your portfolio to determine whether the results meet your expectations and see what can be done if they do not. Continuing to work toward maintaining the original investment goals you set for yourself is essential, and the initial setup of your account is only a first step toward achieving them.

Within each asset class, you can invest in an enormous number of securities. The major classes, such as stocks, bonds, and mutual funds, have already been discussed. In addition, there are index funds, actively managed funds, annuities, and others. Depending on the constituents of these funds, investments in them might fall completely in one asset class or might provide some elements of two or more classes. Choosing securities with which you have some familiarity is useful when investing. The famous investor, Warren Buffett, is a perfect example of this because his company, Berkshire Hathaway, owns shares of Geico Insurance, Dairy Queen, Fruit of the Loom, Procter & Gamble, Coca-Cola, and Anheuser-Busch, among other well-known companies.

There are several ways to buy individual equities. If you are comfortable making your own choices and only want a broker to facilitate a transaction, many online brokerages will charge little for their services. If you want someone to discuss your choices with and help you select between seemingly equivalent companies, you might prefer the expertise of a full-service broker even though the trading will cost you a little more. The extra you spend on the advice of a broker or a financial advisor might be returned by making a superior selection.

However, owning individual shares is not the only way in which you can invest in the stock and bond markets. Another way to buy securities is through a diversified fund, which holds investments in a number of companies. There are many such funds, so you should be able to find one that invests in the companies that interest you. You can select a fund that meets your financial needs, risk tolerance, and investment expertise.

Depending on your previous financial experience, the term fund might be new to you even if you might be aware of the idea of purchasing securities or investment companies. A fund refers to an investment company that is publicly or privately owned and exists to pool money from many different investors to purchase securities.

The most popular type of fund is probably an open-ended no load mutual fund. *These terms are explained in more detail in Chapter 10.* However, an alternative to a mutual fund that is starting to gain in popularity is the exchange-traded fund (ETF). Many advocate for ETFs, and it looks as though they will continue to grow in popularity, but mutual funds still have a place in a well-balanced portfolio and possess their own advantages over ETFs.

The chief distinction between a mutual fund and an ETF is the value of an ETF can vary from the underlying value of the securities in the fund because of market action. The value of a mutual fund is always related back to the securities it owns less any liabilities, and that is the price you will pay for shares in the fund. Either type of fund can be passively managed or actively managed, but the range of actively managed ETFs available is not as wide because they have been available for a shorter period of time.

Because of this, mutual funds are the most common of all pooled investments. Within these funds, you can find a variety of different securities, including stocks, bonds, and money market instruments, which allows investors to diversify as much as they require. It otherwise would be difficult to achieve such a widespread diversification if you had a small portfolio and a restricted amount of investment capital.

Mutual funds, unlike equities and ETF shares, allow you to invest in fractional amounts. Most securities require you to purchase a whole number of shares, but mutual funds do not have this limitation. This means they are more flexible for the small investor. You can add to them with regular monthly payments of a predetermined amount instead of odd sums each month. Unlike many other types of funds, mutual funds will accept investments in small amounts for their purchase.

The flexibility of mutual funds extends to cashing the shares. If you need immediate cash, you can redeem the shares you own at the current net asset value less any fees and charges on any day of the week. Most mutual funds also offer excellent diversification in different companies and market sectors, which reduces the market risk. As an investor, you have little you need to do because the mutual fund manager takes care of all the work necessary to research opportunities. This is much easier than selecting your own equity investments.

Mutual funds will give you the option to receive dividends from your stocks or income from your bonds in cash or reinvest the money into the fund. When you choose to have all your income and dividends reinvested, the compounding effect ensures your fund holding grows substantially. Investors who choose to take this action rather than receive cash payments are not charged additional fees.

Mutual funds have some differences and disadvantages compared to individual equities. Investors are always charged annual fees although these might be as little as 0.5 percent. Some funds charge other expenses, but you generally would not have a good reason to select those funds. Mutual funds also generate distributions each year that are subject to taxes, but with equities, you are only liable for capital gains taxes on the realized gains when you finally sell. Of course, this only defers the tax payments, and you might prefer to pay each year rather than face a lump sum later. However, with a mutual fund, you have no control over how much the distributions are.

Unlike ETFs, mutual funds do not allow you to check the value of your holding during the trading day. Mutual funds are only valued after the markets close, and the net asset value (NAV) is calculated from the closing prices of the assets in the fund.

One advantage of using mutual funds in your portfolio is they are available in a variety of categories and can correspond to different asset classes. Money market mutual funds correspond to cash equivalents, bond mutual funds behave like fixed income investments, stock mutual funds are equity investments, and real estate and commodities-based mutual funds fall into the alternative asset classification.

Because major funds correspond to these various asset classes, the risk and return characteristics are similar to the different characteristics of those classes. You can also find mutual funds that combine several asset classes and allow you to invest in different classes at the same time. Within each class of mutual fund, you can choose funds that correspond to different amounts of risk, including conservative, moderate, or aggressive.

When you review the performance of each fund, bear in mind past performance will not necessarily continue. You should particularly note if the fund manager has changed during the last few years because the character of the fund might vary. However, you should get a good idea of whether the fund has a high volatility and is therefore unsuitable for portfolios that are aimed for short-term goals.

Index funds are available in both mutual funds and exchange-traded funds with the characteristics of each. An index fund follows a generally passive strategy of investing and does not seek to beat the market but simply to follow it. In its simplest form, a manager would buy shares in every company in the index in the right proportions, and the fund would track the index closely, For pragmatic reasons, the fund manager might choose to simply ensure the fund contains shares from each market sector in the correct proportions on the basis that similar shares should have comparable performances.

There are many indices available, including the S&P 500, the NASDAQ, the Dow Jones Industrial Average, and those on world markets. When choosing between indices, select one that suits how aggressive you choose your portfolio to be, and you could blend different indices to match a moderate portfolio if necessary.

So that an index fund can emulate the index itself, the fund should have a low expense ratio. Any drift in value from the index is called a tracking error. The information on the fund's expense ratio and tracking error are available in the fund's prospectus and on the company's website. Although expense ratio is easy to find, the tracking error might be more difficult to find. Instead of tracking error, some funds choose to show the correlation of the fund with its index instead. They might also choose to show the comparison between the various annual returns of the fund and its index. Over time, you will notice the annual return of the fund is less than the index because of fees. If the fund has a high correlation, greater than 95 percent for example, with annual returns close to one another, the fund's tracking error will be low.

In contrast to the passive index fund, actively managed funds are investments for which the fund manager's specific goal is to outperform a benchmark index. The manager achieving his or her goal does not necessarily mean the returns from the fund will be good. If the index loses 20 percent one year and the fund only loses 10 percent, the manager will have outperformed the index and consider his or her job well-done. Fund managers are more concerned with proving their performance relative to similar fund managers because this is the gauge by which new investors are attracted.

Disappointingly, actively managed funds rarely outperform the benchmark index for a prolonged period of time. In many cases, after expenses are considered, the funds underperform the index on a consistent basis. One reason is actively managed funds necessarily have attached to them higher fees than index funds to pay for the advisors and the commission costs of frequent trading. This recurring additional expense has an impact on the returns.

Another increasingly popular type of fund is called a target or life cycle fund. These are intended to be the one and only solution for an investor. Management takes care of the amount of risk the fund incurs. With these funds, the investor decides on a target date related to the year of retirement. After the fund manager determines the initial asset allocation, it is automatically adjusted to be more conservative as the investor grows older and the target date approaches. These funds might also invest in other active or passive funds, and they are popular in 401(k) plans because they simplify the investor's choices by connecting asset allocation to the year of retirement. Although this can be helpful for those who do not feel comfortable choosing their own asset allocation strategies and rebalancing their portfolios, incorporating them into a planned asset allocation portfolio is hard because of the varying risk such funds present over time.

Another choice is investing in REITs for a real estate component in your portfolio, and in many ways, this is better than owning individual real estate because it diversifies your holding and ensures you do not get involved in management problems.

Annuities

If you were interested in a guarantee of steady returns suitable for a conservative investor, you could consider buying an annuity. An annuity is certain although it is considered a costly option. These are designed for investors who are unable or unwilling to assume any kind of risk. The fees are higher on annuities than on other investment choices, but because they are free of risk, they are the preferred choice for investors who are skeptical about stocks, bonds, mutual funds, and alternative investments. Strictly speaking, annuities should not be considered investments because they are products of the insurance industry rather than the investment sector.

Insurance companies offer annuities and provide payments to the investor for a guaranteed period of time in exchange for a premium the investor pays to the annuity provider. The annuity payments you receive might be for a fixed or variable period of time, and you can purchase a life annuity that pays you for the rest of your life. The payments might begin immediately after you purchase the annuity or can be deferred until a specific time, such as retirement.

Once you purchase an annuity, you will not see your capital again. This is not like investing in bonds, which return the capital at the end of the term. The insurance company takes a view on your expected lifespan in determining what the regular payments are compared with the annuity cost. Some annuities can continue for a fixed period of time regardless of the death of the principal holder, and other annuities have a survivorship option that continues payments until both partners are deceased.

Unlike regular investments, annuities' income and capital gains are not taxed as they occur. Only a portion of the payments you receive from your annuity is counted as taxable income. The remainder is considered repayment of the principal you put down. Some investors believe the tax-deferred benefit is well worth the additional cost of the annuity. If you are considering taking out an annuity, make sure you fully understand the costs associated with it, the amount of time you are locked into the annuity, and the guarantees that are available.

Chapter 9:
How Are You Doing?

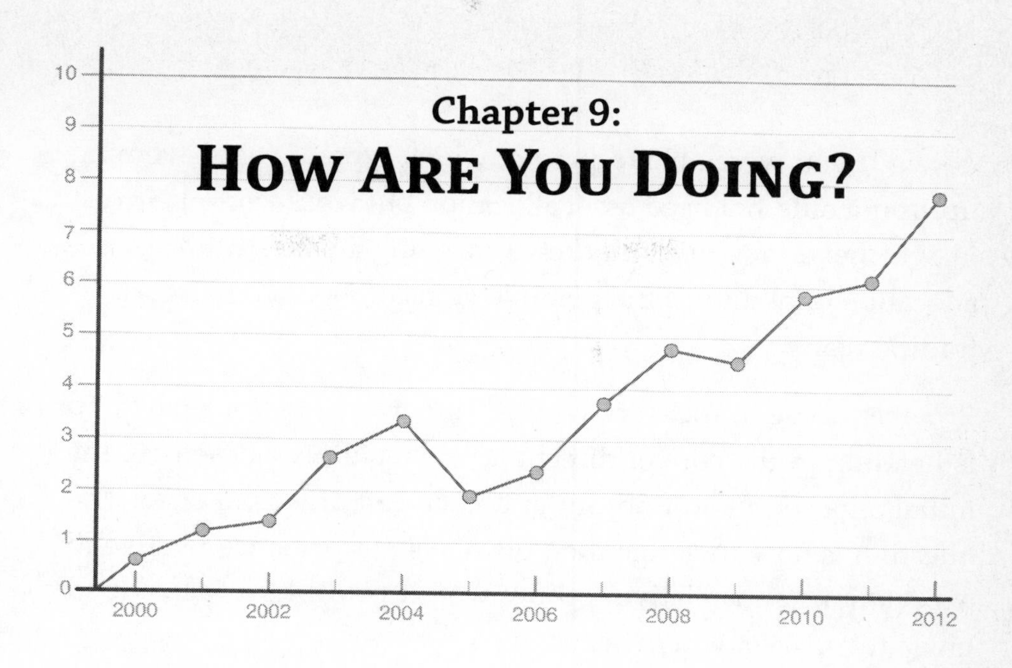

ASSET ALLOCATION IS A CONTINUING PROCESS. PORTFOLIO rebalancing is designed to reinstate the asset allocation you selected for your portfolio and with which you should achieve your targets over the years. However, setting the percentages back to the initial selection is only part of looking after your portfolio because it presupposes your initial selection has been in every way the best for you and your circumstances have not changed.

Despite the hard work that goes into the initial asset allocation, how will you know whether the percentages that have been calculated are going to work out for you? The answer to this is not easy and certainly is not definitive. Underlying all our work on portfolio management is the basic truth that the market for whichever financial securities you've invested in is unpredictable. During some years, stocks go up greatly. Sometimes, they go down. If you were able to predict which type of year is coming up, you would not need asset allocation but would simply invest in whichever way the market was going in the future. Asset allocation only dilutes the possible gains of a perfectly informed trading plan.

It makes sense to measure your results to ensure your portfolio is heading in the correct direction. Don't simply perpetuate the initial allocation and find out at a later date it was in error. The question is how to gauge the portfolio's performance relative to expectations and relative to how well it could have performed given the market you invested in.

As an example, suppose a colleague tells you he made $5,000 in the markets. Although it sounds as though he had invested wisely, find out about a number of factors before deciding whether this performance indeed was exceptional. One of the most basic elements is the amount of money he put at risk by investing in the market. A second fundamental is how long it took for this profit to accumulate. For instance, if he had invested $100,000 five years ago and had only made $5,000 to date, you might change your mind and think the performance of the investment was not poor.

You would also judge how good the investment was in terms of what the general market was doing during that time and which level of risk was involved. Was there a chance of losing half the principal, or was the amount invested always safe?

So, when it comes to evaluating your new asset allocated portfolio and its performance, consider a number of parameters to determine whether it is on track. Making a good return one year does not mean you made the best choices with your investments, particularly if others are making more money. If you have a poor return or a loss on another year, your asset allocation might be to blame, or the markets might have punished everyone. What you need is a process to standardize your return and compare it to a public benchmark that gives you an indication of what you should have earned.

The starting point for assessing how good your gains were is the amount of principal you invested. One of the best ways to evaluate a return you made on your principal is to express it as a percentage per year. Any profit or losses you receive in 12 months can be expressed as a percentage of the amount invested, and this standardizes your return so you can compare it to your colleague's investments and to other market returns.

Depending on the type of investment you have, you might find you have both capital growth and income. Capital growth covers any increase in value of your financial security and can be negative if your investment lost value. Income from an investment might simply be interest payments and can be the dividend yield if you are invested in equities. You must combine both growth and income to see how your results measured up with other investments.

If the length of time you have held the investment is not one year, you need to adjust the returns to allow for this. Using simple averaging, the annual return would be twice what you would have received if you had only held it for six months; if you have held the investments two years, your annual rate of profit is only half of your gains.

Simple averaging is not the only way to calculate your returns, and it is more accurate to compound the values. If you have a savings account, you probably know compound interest multiplies your gains faster than adding on simple interest each year because you start receiving interest on interest after the first period. It is an easy calculation with the help of a calculator because it involves finding the power of the number, which you can do with a financial or scientific calculator.

After you standardize your portfolio's returns, you need something to compare them to so you can see whether you are getting the performance you should. For a stock portfolio, you might choose to compare with the figures for the S&P 500 index because this would give you the level of return you would expect from a fully invested market portfolio. Many more indices are available, but the S&P 500 is a benchmark covering the performance of 500 of the largest traded companies. Choose to compare the performance to the S&P Small Cap 600 index if your portfolio concentrates on smaller companies, and if you have a blended selection of stock sizes, you could choose to combine these two indices in a similar ratio as a benchmark of how your portfolio is performing.

Similarly, if you have bonds in your portfolio, you can choose a bond index to see how the performance of your investments compares to the market. A predominance of bonds in your portfolio indicates you are conservative in your allocation. One major index, which used to be called the Lehman Aggregate Bond Index but has now been taken over by Barclays since Lehman's demise, is considered to be the best total market bond index, and 90 percent of investors use it as a reference. This index includes government-backed securities, mortgage-backed securities, asset-backed securities and corporate bonds, and maturity is longer than one year. It is now called the Barclays Capital U.S. Aggregate Bond Index. Many other indices from Barclays cover emerging and global markets and more specific bonds, such as five- to 10-year government bonds.

To see how your portfolio is behaving relative to the general market, you can choose to use either of these indices or another that is more appropriate to your holdings. Your portfolio will likely include a mix of stocks and bonds, so you can proportion between the indices to see what would be a reasonable return for your ratios. Doing this exercise provides an important check on the dependability of your portfolio selections. A stock or bond index is well-diversified and lowers the risk in this way just as your asset allocation exercise has done. If your portfolio is significantly underperforming the general market, you know you have to review and fix any problems.

CASE STUDY: ASSET ALLOCATION: THE MOST IMPORTANT ASPECT OF INVESTING

Jerry A. Miccolis, CFA®, CFP®, FCAS, MAAA
Co-author of Asset Allocation For Dummies® (Wiley, May 2009)
Principal, chief investment officer, and senior financial advisor
Brinton Eaton Wealth Advisors
One Giralda Farms, Suite 130
Madison, NJ 07940
Phone: 800-364.2468
Fax: 973-292.0003
www.brintoneaton.com

Jerry A. Miccolis holds the Chartered Financial Analyst® (CFA) designation, is a Certified Financial Planner™ (CFP) practitioner, and is a fellow of the Casualty Actuarial Society (FCAS). He also is a member of the American Academy of Actuaries (MAAA), the Financial Planning Association (FPA), and the New York Society of Security Analysts (NYSSA). Miccolis received a bachelor's degree in mathematics from Drexel University. Miccolis specializes in financial planning, risk management, investment research, and portfolio management.

Based in Madison, New Jersey, Brinton Eaton is a boutique advisory firm with a long history of serving individuals and their families across multiple generations. The firm helps its clients protect, grow, administer, and ultimately transfer their legacy of wealth through a full range of integrated services, including lifetime cash flow projections; financial, tax, estate, and retirement planning; investment management; charitable giving; and business succession planning. Brinton Eaton's clients tend to be corporate *executives, professionals, entrepreneurs, and retirees with investable assets more than $2 million. For more information, visit* ***www.brintoneaton.com.***

Asset allocation is important for individual investors to consider because the single most important driver of the performance of any investment portfolio is its asset allocation. Repeated studies have shown asset allocation is significantly more consequential in determining investment results than any other factor, such as stock picking or market timing.

An asset allocation strategy has the following benefit. A portfolio designed according to asset allocation precepts will tend to deliver better long-term returns than any other portfolio with similar risk. Equivalently, such a portfolio will tend to have less risk than any other portfolio with similar expected returns.

Asset allocation and diversification are different. There are no formal, universally accepted definitions of either term, but in popular usage, diversification refers to not confining your investments to one or a small number of individual investments. Asset allocation refers to a much broader, deeper, and richer scientific approach that seeks to identify various asset classes, such as stocks, bonds, real estate, and commodities, that are not positively correlated with each other and mix them together in optimal proportions to achieve a desired risk/return profile for the portfolio. You can be diversified but not well allocated — the reverse is not true.

When you consider whether asset allocation might not work, ask yourself, "Compared to what?" There are certainly market conditions in which asset allocation will not protect you from loss. For example, there have been rare periods when virtually all asset classes moved down together at once. In such a market, in which uncorrelated assets suddenly become closely correlated on the downside, even the best diversified and allocated portfolio will not escape loss. Of course, this did not mean asset allocation didn't work. Asset allocation is not designed to protect a portfolio from loss in every situation; it is designed to create a portfolio that has the best expected return for a given level of risk. Equivalently, it has the lowest risk for a given level of expected return. To get back to the initial question, "Compared to what?," and with apologies to Winston Churchill, asset allocation is worlds better than whatever is in second place despite the flaws it might have.

An investor must consider several things when developing an asset allocation strategy. There is no single correct asset allocation suitable for everyone — it depends on each investor's circumstances. Those circumstances include:

- Investment horizon
- Return objectives
- Risk tolerance
- Cash flow needs
- Retirement benefits
- Tax situation
- Estate planning and asset protection considerations
- Constraints and other special circumstances, such as, avoiding certain investments based on religious beliefs or social concerns and adhering to restrictions on selling company stock

That is why we at Brinton Eaton recommend determining your asset allocation in the context of your financial plan.

Portfolio rebalancing works to restore a portfolio to its intended asset allocation mix. Rebalancing is sometimes a forgotten aspect of asset allocation, but it is quite important. Once your asset allocation drifts away from its intended mix by more than a pre-set amount because of market forces, you should rebalance your portfolio back to target. You do this by selling some, not the entire positions, of your leaders and investing the proceeds in the laggards. You basically take some of your winnings off the table and redeploy them elsewhere. A popular tolerance band is plus or minus 20 percent of your allocation percentage; for example, if you allocate 10 percent of your portfolio to real estate, you rebalance when it drifts lower than 8 percent or higher than 12 percent.

This is much more than a housekeeping chore. Over time, it will produce more return with less risk, and that is the closest thing to a free lunch you will find in investing. It does this by imposing a discipline on you to systematically buy low and sell high in small amounts over and over again.

We currently have about 250 clients at Brinton Eaton. We literally have 250 different portfolios with their own asset allocations because of the importance of determining asset allocation in the context of an investor's financial plan. For example, we might use tax-exempt bonds in taxable accounts for clients in high income tax brackets if we expect the after-tax performance to be superior in that case to taxable bonds. We might favor short-duration bonds in accounts that require greater liquidity, and we might favor high-dividend stocks in accounts that require high current income. For certain clients, we avoid industry sectors that conflict with their religious beliefs. We manage this diversity by doing our own extensive modeling of many different asset classes and deriving broad guideline allocations across a range of different risk profiles. We then identify the client's most appropriate profile and fine-tune the allocation to the client's specific circumstances. For each client, we would have developed a long-term financial plan.

Whether asset allocation could hurt an investor's portfolio returns depends on what you compare asset allocation to. Putting your money under a mattress will protect it from market forces. However, for most investors with any realistic investment horizon, their biggest enemy is not short-term market fluctuation, it is inflation. And safe investments, such as the mattress or insured CDs, are virtually guaranteed to lose purchasing power over the long term. Most investors therefore need "risky" investments to protect themselves from the ravages of inflation over their lifetimes, and asset allocation represents the most enlightened way to invest.

The efficient frontier is an extremely useful device with which to observe and analyze various portfolio choices. Henry Markowitz introduced the concept in 1952 when he developed what is called Modern Portfolio Theory. However, many users of this device have not incorporated useful, and in my view necessary, enhancements that have become accessible during the several decades since its introduction. For example:

- The returns for most asset classes can be modeled much more realistically than the simple representations Markowitz used in his original paper and most users still employ. For example, their "fat tails" can be easily modeled.
- The risk of the various asset classes can be measured much more meaningfully than by the popular standard deviation measure. For example, downside risk is what matters, and it can be easily incorporated.
- The interrelationships among the asset classes are much richer and more interesting than simple static correlations can capture. These relationships can be modeled in ways few users employ.

In short, the basic conceptual framework of MPT — and its signature device, the efficient frontier — remain relevant, but few practitioners are using it in a meaningful way.

Rebalancing

Having paid so much attention to carefully selecting the asset classes and particular investments to make up a portfolio that suits your circumstances, your work is not over. While you own the portfolio, your work will never finish because your investments are always in a state of flux and the portfolio of investments is dynamic. This is apart from any change in direction you might find necessary due to changes in circumstances, which is mentioned in a later part of the chapter.

In the long run, all the investments in a well-diversified portfolio should generate at least a minimal rate of return for the investor. The anticipated rate of return for each part of the portfolio is related to the specific level of risk. All investors expect a higher rate of return from those assets with a higher level of risk; otherwise, there would be no point investing in those asset classes. The problem with this line of thinking is long-term estimates for anticipated returns do not help with short-term projections, particularly where the asset classes are volatile and unpredictable. Some of the investments might perform quite well, and others might exhibit poor performance and not reach the level of return that is expected on average.

It would be easy to build the perfect portfolio if you had knowledge in advance of how each investment will perform. In the real world, it is difficult for an investor to know in advance when each of the securities will move up or down and by how much. If such knowledge were available, the markets would cease to function in a normal way because no one would want to invest in securities they knew would not perform well.

However, because we do not know how certain assets will perform, changing asset classes based on short-term market projections is not good judgement. This technique might work for a while, but it would fail eventually and probably cost more than you made by moving the investments for the short term.

This brings us to the distinct difference between asset allocation and asset diversification, and this is the regular rebalancing of assets within the portfolio. Rebalancing allows the investor to return the portfolio to the original asset allocation target, and in turn, this allows it to retain the position adequate diversification. The simple way to accomplish this is to sell any portion of the portfolio that is in excess of the target allocation and buy additional investments to compensate for those that are below the target allocation.

The main principle is that your portfolio might need rebalancing because the proportions of securities will drift away from their allocations over time. This is needed because the investments are selected to minimize correlation or even have negative correlation so they will not all go up or down together. Therefore, the proportions between them will vary and might need to be adjusted back to the desired levels. This presupposes that the levels you have set for your portfolio in the first place are correct and efficient, but this would be a reasonable assumption based on all the work you would have done to establish them for your circumstances.

One principle you must understand to see the purpose of rebalancing is that of reversion to mean. This theory simply states that you expect the assets' investment returns to come back to the historical average levels. If the asset has generated returns above the average level, it will also generate returns that are lower at some time. It might not be possible to say whether the returns will remain high for one more year or five more years, but the expectation is that the returns should be lower to balance back to the historical average. Rebalancing allows the investor to take advantage of overly optimistic and overly pessimistic price variations within the marketplace, and the discipline of rebalancing forces the sale of any portion of the portfolio that has increased in value and the purchase of desired assets that have fallen in value.

Rebalancing also reasserts the proportions you have blended along with their correlation factors to create a portfolio that has a reduced risk. If the proportions have drifted away from your calculated values by concentrating in one particular asset class, such as equities, your risk would drift toward the risk of the asset class rather than remain low. Rebalancing is taking precaution to maintain the reduction in risk.

In other words, if you do not attend to your portfolio on a regular basis, it will end up with a higher risk than you intended. Although the riskier investments are those that might offer a higher rate of return, they throw your portfolio back to the problem of timing rather than keep a smooth and steady growth. The portfolio is optimized to reduce risk and increase return on average when it is at its target percentages. A concentrated asset class might work well for a time but will also lay you open to losses or at least reduced portfolio returns.

How it works

There are different ways to rebalance. Some of them re-establish with precision your selected proportions of asset classes, and some are based on a "near enough" scheme, which avoids excessive trading and costs at the expense of accuracy. Either way, the idea is to sell some of the growing assets and buy some of the also-rans with the proceeds. Only in this way can you re-establish the balance between the asset classes.

It sounds rational, but you will find that this is sometimes difficult to do. It means you will have to sell some of your best performing investments in the hottest sectors that your investing friends might still be excited about and instead pick up more of the financial instruments that have been letting you down by losing value or gaining less than others. If you are concerned about your ability to do this, your only consolation is that probability science will prove you right in the long run. Unless your friends are also interested in asset allocation, it certainly is best to avoid telling your them exactly what you are doing because they might think you lost your mind.

On the other hand, rebalancing takes away any possibility of having to time the markets, which is notoriously difficult to do without significant study and knowledge, and relies on statistics to win out in the long run.

The theory of rebalancing is the essence of the modern portfolio theory. By diversifying assets within classes that are dissimilar and by restoring those investments to their original target asset allocation as needed, you reduce your portfolio's volatility while increasing your returns.

Advantages and disadvantages

Although following an asset allocation model requires you to rebalance to retain the benefits, you always have a choice to change your portfolio or continue holding what you started with despite the imbalance that built up. Therefore, a quick look at the specific advantages and disadvantages of rebalancing is helpful.

The main advantage of rebalancing is it increases the chances that you will achieve the returns you expect from your portfolio for the given asset allocation in the long term. This is because you are rebalancing the returns of the different asset classes and you control the risk down to the level calculated for your asset allocation. You are not allowing a specific asset class to become concentrated and taking more of a chance the outcome will be as you anticipate. Another advantage of rebalancing when required is it makes you pay more attention to the financial securities and involves you in your portfolio. Sometimes, a security might not be performing as well as expected for the asset class, and rebalancing would make you aware of this.

There are some disadvantages with rebalancing, particularly if you do not apply sensible parameters when you do it. It is possible you could rebalance too frequently, which would cause high transaction costs, possible tax implications, and a waste of time. Another disadvantage, which might be out of your control, is that some of the more poorly performing investments of which you increase your holding might not revert to the average in a reasonable amount of time. The nature of the securities or the asset class as a whole might change to different risk and reward expectations. Finally, it can be difficult to go against the flow and dispose of assets that are performing well and buy losers. But because this is the equivalent of buying low and selling high, it is something that should be pursued.

When to rebalance

If you rebalance too frequently, you will incur higher transaction costs, possibly payable taxes, and certainly take up time. Although rebalancing is not intended to help with market timing, if you do it too often you will be selling rising assets before they reach their peak and buying falling assets while they are still on the way down.

On the other hand, if you rebalance too infrequently, any winners you had in your portfolio might lose value before you get to them. Asset allocation requires you to take an active interest in your portfolio to retain the risk and reward advantages.

Because you cannot know the movements of the market in advance, it might not be optimal to apply rebalancing on a fixed schedule, such as once a year or once a quarter. However, rebalancing on a schedule is preferred to not rebalancing at all. If you do not have the time or perseverance to watch your portfolio, it is best to schedule rebalancing about three times a year depending on the volatility of your investments.

Some investors will rebalance according to changes in value of the securities, such as plus or minus 5 percent or 10 percent, and this is likely to be more effective than rebalancing by calendar. Another method involves updating a spreadsheet analysis of your holdings and rebalancing if any of the asset classes drift more than 5 percent away from the target allocation. Rebalancing in response to the performance of the portfolio might not, in reality, take much more time than rebalancing on a set schedule because in some years there will be little volatility and probably little need to rebalance. If you find this method causes you to rebalance every month or so, you might need to revisit the percentages you allow the values to drift because the costs of frequent trading will negatively affect you.

Rebalancing a portfolio based on percentage strategy tends to provide higher returns with less portfolio risk than using a calendar method. However, this strategy does take more time to implement and monitor, particularly when starting out. For this reason, percentage strategy might not be the best for an individual investor to use. A calendar method is simpler and might be more cost-effective for the individual investor. Although you can expect the returns to be slightly lower, you must balance this against the cost of monitoring a portfolio.

Choosing the calendar method of rebalancing is therefore much simpler than the percentage method. If you use this way, you simply set a date at what you consider to be an appropriate interval, and make sure you review your portfolio on that date for any needed adjustments. Those who choose the percentage method to trigger rebalancing necessarily have to spend more time, and review the portfolio more often.

How to rebalance

Although you might think it is necessary to adjust the percentages of each of the asset classes back to the starting point, it is possible to take a pragmatic attitude to rebalancing and just bring the percentages back within your allowed ranges. There might be some problems with trying to rebalance to the initial figures.

The main purpose of rebalancing is to reduce positions that have become concentrated because of growth. If your portfolio contains some alternative investments, you might find it difficult to include them in the rebalancing because of illiquidity. Even if you are determined to accurately rebalance the rest of the funds, be prepared to accept some drift from the original percentage for such assets.

There are no hard and fast rules about how deeply you go into rebalancing. Any amount of rebalancing will improve the portfolio and give you an advantage over a simple buy and hold investment strategy. When rebalancing, you should concentrate on the funds and assets that are specifically outside the range of values you have set and worry less about those that have drifted but are still within bounds. In this way, you can minimize the number of trades you undertake and avoid compromising the advantages you seek from asset allocation. The allocation percentages are derived from generalities and averages, which means the 2 percent extra drift you leave untouched in the mid-cap securities could go up or down and just as easily work for as against you.

Dealing with Life Events

Rebalancing your portfolio is something that needs to be done at regular intervals that depend on the volatility of your investments. However, circumstances sometimes can change to make you to reconsider the fundamental basis of your portfolio rather than simply reinstate it to the original concept. You can expect to have to change the basis at some point in the future, but situations could force you to change without much warning.

For instance, you might retire early. This could be a planned event, or you might be unfortunate enough to find you are laid off later in life with little prospect of securing further employment. Either way, you need to go back to the strategy phase of your asset allocation and make modifications so you can project possible outcomes. Although a forced layoff might produce changes in your expectations for retirement, the planning you have done up to this point allows you to see how you have to modify your plans and whether you can find a sustainable lifestyle that will suit you.

Even if you have been involuntarily removed from the workforce, you have choices for going forward with your life. Increasingly, people are finding they can work in ways that interest them after leaving their career. Sometimes, they increase their activity in a hobby and find ways to use it to supplement their reduced income. Others find a part-time job locally is financially and intellectually satisfying. Factor all these into your planning to gauge the effect.

Another choice you have is when to start drawing social security payments. Although they can be claimed starting at the age of 62, this will fix them as a substantially lower amount than if you waited until full retirement age. However, the option exists. One little-known fact is you can draw social security early but reinstate it to the full value later by repaying the amount you received.

You do this by filling out a "Request for Withdrawal of Application," which is Form SSA-521 available online. When you file this, it will be as though you had never applied for benefits. You have to repay all the benefits received to date, but social security does not charge interest. You can immediately reapply to receive the benefits due for your current age, and this works out to be a much more effective use of funds you repay than most other choices. It certainly gives a better return than buying a life annuity with the cash.

Another option is to start withdrawing funds from your retirement account. This can be done under special circumstances before you reach the required age, but at the age of 59 and a half, anybody can take funds from their retirement account without penalty.

Another life event occurring at a younger age is starting a family. This might be planned, but it could certainly make you reconsider how you want your portfolio positioned for the coming years. A family makes financial impacts in every area of your life, and these include not just the obvious one of increased cost of living. There might be babysitting costs or the hidden costs from one partner's inability to keep full-time employment. Having a family might force you to buy a larger house, change your vacation plans, and save for college costs.

Your approach can be the same as you modify your calculations to encompass the new event. Go back to your original strategy, examine the reasons and assumptions that established the current direction, and if appropriate, modify to see where you have to make adjustments.

On a less desirable note, another important life change is divorce. With all the questions surrounding filing for maintenance, awarding custody of the children, and deciding who gets the house, you should not overlook the changes it might require to your portfolio strategy. Any subsequent remarriage forces another strategy review.

Finally, another life change you might not anticipate at the moment is a change of career. Spending 20 or 30 years at the same job could leave you yearning for more fulfillment, and a change of career late in life often will mean a radical income adjustment. You sometimes will even go back to school to train for the new career, and you will be faced with fees for tuition and other costs apart from the loss of income.

Consider your asset allocation and your portfolio as a living document, not something frozen on the day you agreed to it with your financial advisor. There will be always be changes, and you need to adapt your plans even in the best situation.

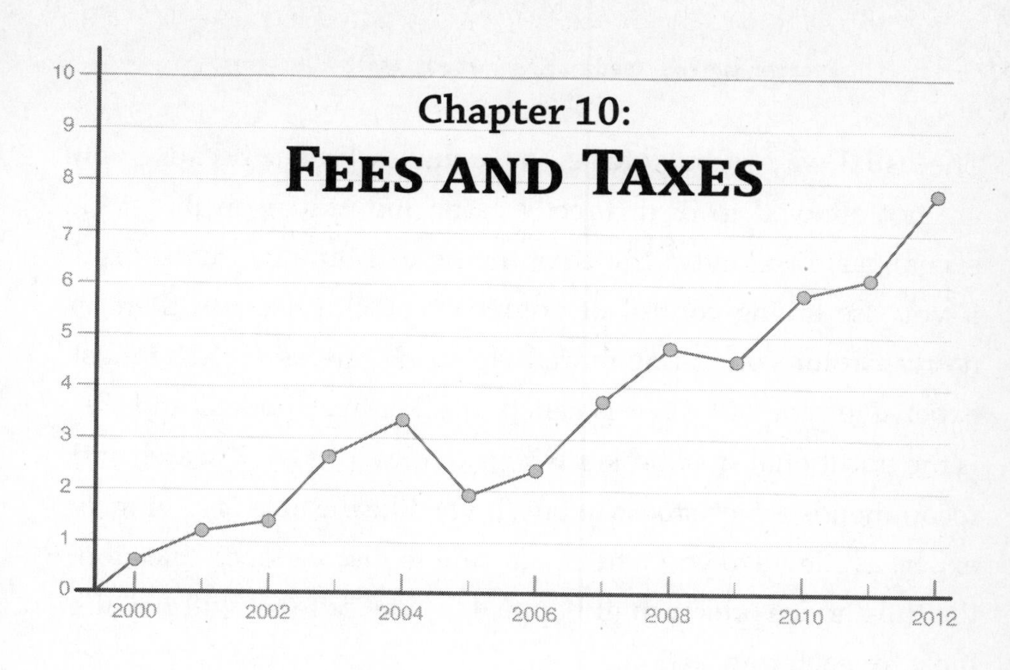

Chapter 10:
Fees and Taxes

INEVITABLY, IT COSTS SOMETHING TO DO ANYTHING, AND investing in various securities is no exception. In this chapter, we look at the various ways you can buy securities and minimize your expenses. Paying more than you need to implement your plan will adversely affect your returns, so you want to find the most economical way to take up the equity positions you have decided on.

Fees

One of the earliest decisions you must make is whether to invest in individual securities or select a fund that diversifies your investment among different securities with the same characteristics. Low investment fees help to make your asset allocation plan successful.

The usual way to buy stocks is through a broker because you are not allowed to deal directly as an individual on the stock exchanges. You have a choice of the type of broker you use, and if you are taking control of your own stock selection, there is no reason for you to pay more than strictly necessary. The most expensive type of broker is called a full-service broker, and this is the traditional stockbroker who provides internal research and recommends which stocks to buy. If you like the idea of having an expert available to you when you want to discuss stock selection, the full-service broker might appeal to you, but you will pay the most for each transaction.

The opposite of this is called a discount broker. You should expect to make your own investment decisions if you use one of these. That said, many of these brokers are providing more facilities, including reports and news feeds about different companies, so the amount of information available is growing. If you are happy doing your own research on different companies and making a selection within the asset class, a discount broker is all you need, and you can save on the commissions and fees.

A spinoff from the discount broker, the premium discount broker provides a middle ground. There is no hard and fast rule about what makes a premium discount broker, but a company like Charles Schwab provides more support in terms of information and office visits and charges a little more commission than a discount broker.

If you go to your broker for some advice, be warned they do not have to give you unbiased, independent recommendations. Some brokers will churn your account, or recommend frequent trading, solely to inflate the commissions. You would hope not to encounter this if you stuck to the major brokers.

You might have heard of an alternative to using a stockbroker, which involves dealing directly with some companies that allow investors to buy stocks directly from them. This method has some advantages, and you can often set up a purchase scheme to buy stocks at regular intervals in small quantities. If commissions are charged, they are less than a broker would require. However, using this method is not as instant as buying through a broker, so you cannot take advantage of a sudden dip in the price you might see on the markets.

If you choose to invest through mutual funds, a number of fees can be levied. Some of these depend on your choice of fund, so they are considered optional. With careful selection, you will not need to pay them. In particular, some mutual funds charge loads either when you buy into the fund at the front end or sell at the back end. A load simply means a sales commission, which goes to the salesperson or broker involved in the deal.

A load can be as high as 8.5 percent of the purchase price. This is the limit imposed by the Financial Industry Regulatory Authority (FINRA), the organization that regulates securities. This means you would need an increase in value of 9.29 percent to break even. Even if you go directly to the company to purchase the same fund, you will still encounter load charges. The long-standing argument for loads is these funds have better performance than funds without. There is no factual basis for this assertion. The Institute for Econometric Research undertook a 25-year study that found no load funds gave better returns even when loads were not taken into account.

Mutual funds are well-regulated, so you should easily be able to find out the amounts charged for fees and commissions and compare them between funds. Many of these fees fall under the heading of operating expenses. Operating expenses are incurred by all mutual funds and can be found in the fund's prospectus. They are simply the cost of doing business, so they cannot be avoided although they vary from fund to fund.

The operating expenses are expressed as a percentage per year, which varies from a fraction of a percent up to 2 or 3 percent. The higher fees are associated with funds that require more work, such as actively traded funds, and the lower fees apply to passive funds, such as index funds. You should look for an expense ratio of no more than 0.5 percent for a simple money market fund, around 0.75 percent for a simple bond fund, up to 1 percent for a higher yielding bond fund, and up to 1.5 percent for an actively managed stock trading fund.

Included in the operating expenses are management fees, which are the costs for running the office; investment advisory fees, which cover the costs of an investment advisor or management team; audit fees to cover the legal requirement of an independent audit each year; director's fees; SEC fees; report expenses; and occasionally 12b-1 fees, which are not normally charged by a no load fund because they represent the costs of marketing and distribution separate from management fees.

In addition to the annual operating expenses, some funds charge other fees; generally, you do not need to pay these fees. You should make sure to select a fund that does not require them. Some mutual funds levy redemption fees when you sell your shares in the fund. Some believe these fees were created to discourage investors from changing funds frequently, and they are about 0.5 percent of the value you redeem. Some funds now charge a switching fee even when you are switching between mutual funds run by the same company, and this practice could grow. Companies used to allow convenient and free switching between funds in the same family, but it seems a switching fee was introduced to discourage frequent fund changing.

Finally, some mutual funds list separately a maintenance fee. Unless this is for a special reason, such charges should already be included in the operating expenses, so you are advised to steer clear of mutual funds that try to increase their profit through such practices. Regulating authorities require all these additional fees to be made clear in the prospectus, and it is up to you to spot any additional fees before investing.

Taxes: Asset Location

You have already learned the importance of asset allocation and the importance of building a diversified portfolio to increase returns and reduce risk. However, asset allocation is not enough to provide the highest net return for the dollars you invest. All the asset allocation in the world is not going to help unless you learn where to put those assets so they are tax-efficient. Asset allocation involves picking the right mixture of assets, and asset location means learning where to put those assets so you pay the least amount of tax on the returns. In addition to fees, investors need to be aware of the impact of taxation on their portfolio. There are several ways to approach minimizing taxes, and they require that the portfolio is set up in the best way. First, you will have a choice of asset location, or the type of account in which each investment is placed. Some types of account are fully taxable, some allow you to defer taxation, and one is tax-free.

If you hold your assets in an ordinary account, you can expect that any gains will be taxed. There are several choices of tax-deferred accounts, and the ones you are probably most familiar with are individual retirement accounts (IRAs) and 401(k) plans. There is no ongoing taxation on these accounts as long as you do not withdraw any funds, and these accounts are used to hold assets to retirement. The account that allows tax-free growth and tax-free withdrawals is a Roth IRA. This must be funded with after-tax contributions unlike some other retirement accounts, but if you achieve good growth with your investments, it will prove to be the most tax efficient.

The tax situation is relatively straightforward when you are buying and selling equities. The chief consideration is whether the capital gains are long-term or short-term, or whether the security has been held for more than a year or less than a year, because short-term capital gains tax is more expensive.

Your cost basis on the securities is the amount you paid for them, and when you sell them for profit the difference between the buying and selling price is called the realized gain. It is this amount the IRS identifies as a capital gain for tax purposes. If you hold securities that have fallen in value, and you do not see any future holding onto them, you can sell them for a capital loss. This offsets the capital gains and reduces your tax liability.

If your portfolio includes mutual funds, your tax liability might depend on the fund manager's actions and the way the fund is administered. If you are investing in a mutual fund through a retirement account, you can simply select the fund with the best return. Taxes will only be payable on the withdrawals. For funds held outside of a retirement fund, you will be liable for taxes on profits and distributions. If you are in a high tax bracket, you might find tax-free bond funds give you a better return after allowing for the taxes on higher yield funds; in a low tax bracket, tax-free bond funds would probably not give you the yield of taxable funds.

Even if you do not take any distributions from the fund and reinvest them without any trading, you might owe some income tax each year. The distribution reinvestment is the same as being paid by the fund and buying more shares with the proceeds for tax purposes. The fund is required by law to distribute income received from its holdings. If the fund manager has sold any stocks held during the year, there might also be capital gains on which you would be liable for tax.

One way to deal with the taxes is to choose a municipal bond fund. Any income from this fund is free of federal taxes, and if the bond is issued in your state of residence, it probably will be free of state taxes too. However, the rate of return might be lower than other funds.

Another answer fund companies have created is to produce mutual funds that are called tax managed. The manager of a tax-managed fund is charged with making an effort to minimize tax liabilities. For example, he could realize losses from another part of the fund if he sold some shares for a profit. Although there are no guarantees, this type of fund might prove to be more tax efficient if you have already contributed all that is allowed to your retirement accounts.

Taxes can also be a challenge when rebalancing. Together with commissions, they put a practical limit on how often you can rebalance and still make extra gains. The effect of taxes and commissions is frequently underestimated when investors consider how often to rebalance. You can try to mitigate the effect by offsetting gains with any losses in your portfolio. Also, rebalance by putting new money in the underrepresented asset class rather than investing the money in accordance with your asset allocation and buying and selling separately.

Further difficulties with tax management include rebalancing assets held in different accounts, such as retirement accounts. Be aware the ideal tax strategy for this year might not be as efficient in five years because your personal tax rate might change or government action might change the applicable rates.

Your first priority in organizing your portfolio should be asset allocation so you can maximize your returns for an acceptable risk level. Then, you can select the asset locations that best suit the characteristics of the different investments you want to make. Even if you cannot put all the heavily taxable assets into tax-advantaged accounts, bear in mind that the objective is not necessarily to minimize your taxes but to maximize your bottom line returns from the portfolio.

Types of account

One of the first things to do is look at the accounts you have to see where they fit into your contact structure. If you are like the majority of people, you probably have more than one investment account within your family unit. Although they might seem like too many accounts to track, look at the following investment accounts you might not have even considered:

- Employer-provided tax-deferred 401(k) plan
- Personal tax-deferred individual retirement account (IRA)
- Health savings account (HSA), also tax-deferred
- At least one investment account of a taxable nature through a broker or financial advisor

If you are married, you and your spouse might each have one of the above accounts in addition to joint accounts. It is easy to find the number of investment accounts for a married couple run into double digits. You and your spouse might also own a Roth IRA, an account you fund with after-tax dollars that gives you tax-free growth.

Looking at the tax advantages when you are developing your asset allocation strategy is important but does not mean you should not invest in taxable investments. Choose them wisely and place as many as possible into a tax-deferred account. For instance, REITs are extremely taxable, so you might consider putting those investments into a tax-deferred account, such as an IRA, and saving your taxable accounts for those investments that are more tax friendly.

As a guide, the following types of investments are the ones you should consider placing in tax-deferred or tax-free account:

- Corporate bonds and bond funds
- Commodities funds
- REITs and REIT mutual funds
- Mortgages and certificates of deposit
- Any mutual funds that have a high turnover of their holdings

Investments that are more suitable for a taxable account include:

- Municipal bonds and bond funds
- Low turnover funds, including index funds
- Growth stocks because gains will be taxed at the long-term capital gains tax rate if held long enough. In a tax-deferred account, this would instead eventually be taxable at your income tax rate, which is higher.

Most nonretirement investment accounts fall into the taxable account category. In other words, any dividends or capital gains you earn from those accounts are taxable in the year they occur. The following three types of investment accounts are nonretirement and thus fall into the taxable income sector:

- Individual accounts registered to only one owner. They might sometimes be a transfer on death (TOD) account if the original owner has designated a beneficiary in case they die during the time they own the account.
- Joint accounts are owned by husband and wife together though this is not always the case. The two most common types of joint accounts are:
    - Joint tenants with right of survivorship (JTWROS), which means both account holders have equal rights to the assets in the account and survivorship rights. The survivor inherits the entire value of the other member's

share of the account in the event of that person's death. It is possible to have more than two owners on this type of account.

- Tenants in common (TIC) means each account holder has an equal share in the assets of the account and retains his or her share in the event of the death of the other owner(s). There is no automatic transfer of ownership unless those terms are specified in a will. Some states, such as California, consider all assets as community property and do not recognize TIC or JTWROS. If you live in a community property state, you might wish to consider setting up lifetime trusts for yourself and your spouse individually.

- Trusts are set up by one person for the benefit of another. There are several different types of trusts; some you can set up while you are still living, while others are part of an estate that will transfer only upon the death of the person who set up the trust. For more information on trusts and what they entail, you might wish to ask your financial advisor or obtain some information online to suit your needs.

One of the major benefits of tax-deferred accounts, such as 401(k) plans, IRAs, and annuities, is you pay no tax on the account until you begin withdrawing funds. With a tax-free account, such as the Roth IRA, you do not get a tax break when you make deposits to the account, but you will not have to pay any taxes when you begin making withdrawals. With a tax-free HSA, you do not have to pay any taxes at all, but there is a requirement for you to use the money to fund certain health care costs. Some companies also offer a similar account for childcare expenses. Some of the more common tax-deferred and tax-free accounts are as follows:

- A 401(k) is a retirement plan an employer offers that allows employees who contribute to defer a certain percentage of their salaries from taxation. It includes contributions before and after taxes. The legally allowed maximum of contributions before taxes is 6 percent of the employee's salary. Although there are no tax advantages to saving more than 6 percent, none of what you place in the before-tax account is taxed until you withdraw it. The downside to this is that when you withdraw the funds from your 401(k), they are taxed as ordinary income. There are also IRS rules on how much you can contribute to your account each year, which is currently 6 percent, on a before-tax basis. The benefit is that if you leave the company before retirement, you can roll over the funds from your 401(k) plan into an IRA without any tax consequences. An additional advantage to rolling your funds into an IRA is that the fees associated with the 401(k) can be high yet hard to identify; thus, an identical investment in an IRA might provide a higher net return. However, this might not take into account that some companies contribute matching funds to the 401(k), so the loss of these additional funds might reduce any additional return.

- Traditional IRAs are similar to 401(k) plans as far as tax deferral status, contribution limits, and withdrawal requirements. The main difference is you can open an IRA on your own without having to go through an employer.
- Roth IRAs are similar to traditional IRAs but are funded out of after-tax income, which gives you no tax advantages at the time of contribution. However, you do not pay any taxes when you withdraw the funds.
- HSAs are special accounts that allow you to contribute money on a pretax basis. All the money is tax-free as long as it is used to pay qualified medical expenses. These plans are combined with a health care plan that has an associated high deductible amount.
- Annuities provide regular payments for a specific period of time following the payment of premiums to an annuity issuer. The annuity issuer is an insurance company.

STOCKS
BONDS

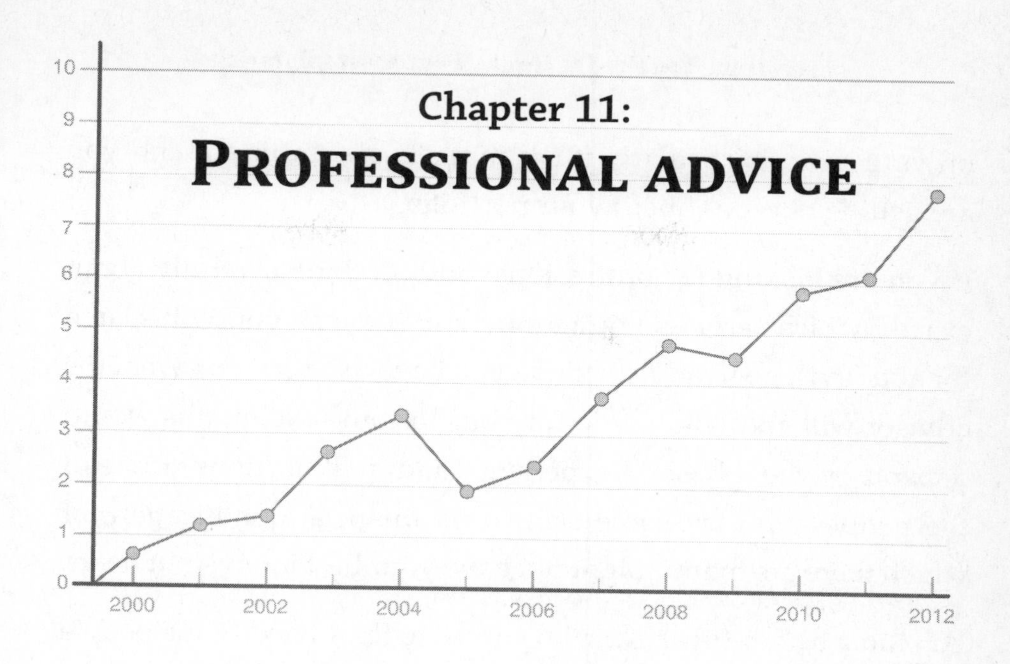

Chapter 11: PROFESSIONAL ADVICE

IF YOU WOULD RATHER NOT MANAGE YOUR OWN PORTFOLIO, one solution would be to hire a finance professional to take care of it. You should expect a competent manager to help you formulate your asset allocation, implement the plan, advise and help when rebalancing is necessary, and help modify asset allocation when your circumstances change.

There are several good reasons you might consider appointing an investment manager to help with your portfolio. First, an experienced manager will be invaluable in knowing their way around the markets and helping you decide and implement your strategies. Second, you should expect the manager to alert you when rebalancing is required, which saves you from having to watch the markets all the time. Third, it can be comforting to talk with a professional rather than try to cope with all circumstances on your own, particularly if the markets are uncertain and you are getting nervous about your portfolio.

If you are looking for professional advice, think carefully about exactly which services you require and the way you will search for and find a good advisor. First, you have to be clear on what the advisor will and will not do for you. To some extent, this would depend on the advisor's experience and qualifications. Some of the people who lay some claim to a financial qualification, of which there are many, might not have your best interests at heart.

You must be careful about who you go to for advice. Some people in the investment business will claim to give you sound advice but be receiving commission from selling particular investment products. Their advice is unlikely to be unbiased, so they might not be best for your portfolio although it is tempting to receive free or low-cost advice from them.

This does not mean you will necessarily get good advice from an advisor who is compensated only by charging you a fee. Although this is the only form of remuneration that guarantees independence, it does not guarantee competence, and you still need to use due diligence on the advisor you are considering. A starting point is to check the background information on a potential advisor at the Securities and Exchange Commission website at **www.sec.gov**.

A financial advisor who is paid through fees will normally suggest a charge based on a percentage of your account's value.

The amounts charged vary widely, but a reasonable level would be about 0.5 percent per year subject to a minimum payment. If a financial advisor you are considering wants to charge much more, you are at liberty to negotiate the price, and this will save you money every year. Make sure you get in writing all fees that will be charged to your account and all ways in which the advisor is paid to make sure there are no conflicts of interest.

Qualifications

There are many different financial qualifications. The number of initials after someone's name is not a guide to their wisdom in handling your financial affairs. As a starting point, here are some of the commonly recognized qualifications you might see. A qualification's exclusion from this list is not intended to imply that it is necessarily inferior, but it is probably less likely to be encountered.

One of the heavyweight qualifications is Chartered Financial Analyst (CFA), which requires passing three exams plus gaining four years of professional experience in the investment world. It is one of the most demanding qualifications for a financial advisor to attain.

Other qualifications worth looking out for are Registered Investment Advisor (RIA) and the associated Investment Advisor Representative (IAR). RIA is most commonly applied to companies although some individuals have this qualification. The professionals who work for an RIA qualified company train for the IAR designation. RIA is a significant designation because the advisors must work in your best interest by law, are covered by the Investment Advisers Act of 1940, and are registered with the SEC as such.

For more general financial planning instead of investment-specific advice, the following two designations are the most widely accepted. The most well-known perhaps is Certified Financial Planner (CFP). This requires a combination of examination, experience, and continuing education. You can check on an individual's qualifications by looking them up on the Certified Financial Planner Board of Standards website **www.cfp.net**.

For help more specific to income tax planning, the designation of Certified Public Accountant (CPA) is highly regarded. This is a State regulated designation that can be checked via on National Association of State Boards of Accountancy website **www.nasba.org**. Click through to the relevant state board.

Whichever type of designation your potential financial advisor has, it should be possible to research with the organization issuing those credentials and see whether there have been any complaints against them. Although it might be preferable to use an advisor with recognized qualifications from a major institution or governing body, you can form an opinion about another designation and see how much learning and experience it requires with some research.

CASE STUDY: MAXIMIZE RETURN WHILE REDUCING RISK

Mike Carpenter
Author: The Risk-Wise Investor: How to Better Understand and Manage Risk
www.riskwiseinvestor.com
Mike@riskwiseinvestor.com
CarpenterAssociates
MikeCarpenter@mcarpenterassoc.com
P.O. Box 306
Concord, MA 01742
Phone: 978-369-5711

Mike Carpenter is a 35-year veteran of the investment business and founder of his own consulting firm, CarpenterAssociates. Although he has always been intrigued by the investment business, he worked his way through college as a medical research lab technician and clinical lab tech and then graduated with a bachelor's degree in biology. After working for a few years as a microbiologist in the pharmaceutical industry, he became interested again in helping investors deal with the ever-changing variety, challenges, and opportunities of investing. After extensive personal research and efforts, he was selected for a financial advisor training program with PaineWebber. That training included a special program at the firm's offices on Wall Street. He graduated from the training program, and after successfully completing all the required securities examinations, he was licensed as a financial advisor a few weeks after the OPEC oil embargo in late 1973.

After many years as a successful financial advisor, he was promoted to regional management, then national level executive management positions in the investment industry. In 2003, he established his own consulting firm and serves financial services industry firms, executives, and advisors.

Asset allocation is important for individual investors to consider because implemented properly, asset allocation will maximize return while reducing risk. Because no one can predict the future, participating in a variety of asset classes reduces investment risk, improves return, and reduces portfolio volatility by taking advantage of the different risk/reward, performance extremes, and performance characteristics of each asset class.

The following benefits are derived from using an asset allocation strategy:

- Gaining exposure to a wider range of possibilities
- Avoiding exposure to any one asset class
- Avoiding the trap of trying to predict the best asset class
- Feeling the comfort that comes with reducing portfolio volatility

Asset allocation is different from diversification because asset allocation is at a higher level than diversifying only within one or two asset classes. Asset allocation requires diversifying among asset classes and then diversifying within each of those asset classes to provide a more complete, multilevel diversification.

There are some times when asset allocation does not work. There occasionally are periods of time, such as major financial crises, when many asset classes will move in tandem. However, as demonstrated in the most recent financial crisis, gold, U.S. government bonds, and cash all held their value. Investors who also allocated some of their asset to those asset classes did better than those who did not.

Even before asset allocation decisions are made, investors must determine which risks they want to avoid, which risks they are willing to accept and manage, and which risks they are willing to accept outright. Once that process is completed, asset allocation decision-making becomes much easier.

It is simplistic to say the risk profile of any investor I work with will match their asset allocation strategy. Because many investors have multiple portfolios with different investment objectives, including retirement, children's education, charitable giving, and gifts to children or grandchildren, the asset allocation strategy should be based on the objective and time frame of each portfolio rather than investor's risk profile.

For instance, it can be entirely appropriate for a retired widow with a portfolio dedicated to the education of her newborn grandchild to have an aggressive asset allocation strategy for that portfolio and a conservative allocation for her core income-producing portfolio.

Portfolio rebalancing works to restore a portfolio to its intended asset allocation. Rebalancing takes advantage of the phenomenon of reversion to the mean. It provides the discipline to trim those asset classes that have outperformed and reinvest the funds in asset classes that have underperformed, which is normally psychologically difficult for investors to do.

Rebalancing is an automatic way to follow the old Wall Street axiom of buying low and selling high and bring any asset class overweighting or underweighting back into balance.

Asset allocation can hurt an investor's portfolio returns, but it will only reduce the returns of investors who have perfect foresight and the capacity to accept increased risks.

Investors who can consistently select and invest in the top asset class and avoid the worst performing asset classes each year will enjoy greater returns with greater risk than investors who allocate assets across the spectrum. The only problem is that few, if any, investors have ever been able to consistently and successfully accomplish that feat over a long period of time.

The next best thing to perfect foresight is to give up prediction and allocate assets across a broad array of asset classes, then periodically rebalance when the asset allocation becomes unbalanced.

Only in a limited way is it correct to say the efficient frontier is an accurate indicator of investor expectations. Over a long-term time horizon of 60 years or longer, the efficient frontier reflects reasonable expectations for institutional investors who have indefinite life expectancies and long time horizons.

However, over shorter term 10-year periods, as demonstrated by a Rydex Investments/Ibbotson decade-by-decade study on "The Inefficient Frontier," the actual efficient frontier changes shape and placement dramatically. It inverted during the first 10 years of the new millennium and flattened in the 1970s. Therefore, individual investors with 5-, 10-, 15-, or 20-year time horizons, who are living and investing in the most rapidly changing period in human history should be cautious about using the efficient frontier of the last 60 years to set their expectations for the next 5, 10, 15, or 20 years.

Interrogations

Regardless of qualifications, you will still need to interrogate potential financial advisors to determine whether their experience is appropriate for your situation and make sure you can work together. If the relationship works out, you might deal with your advisor for many years.

You need to find out whether the advisor offers the services you envision using whether they are buying and selling securities or minimizing your taxes. It is not necessary for your financial advisor to be an expert in all aspects of personal finance as long as his or her expertise covers your areas of interest.

In a similar vein, you should question whether he or she has clients in a situation similar to your own. If the advisor has such a record, ask if you can speak to some of the clients to obtain a personal reference. Some companies limit their involvement in certain aspects or might require you to have a minimum portfolio size for them to consider managing it for you.

If the financial advisor works in a large firm, you will want to ensure he or she is the one who is personally dealing with your account. Make sure your account was not given to a junior member to take care of. You should try to meet all the staff who will be coming into contact with your portfolio.

When it comes to details of the contract you take out with the financial advisor, clarify several variables. For example, know how often you will be sent a progress report on your portfolio and the amount of detail it will contain. Look for a progress report at least every quarter. It should separate each investment, give comparisons with market averages, and include advice about tax liabilities.

Other issues include whether you are tied into a contract with a financial advisor for certain number of years or whether you can terminate the contract at will. The contract might include a discretionary clause that instructs the advisor to make the necessary trades for you. You might only receive advice and have to implement the investments.

CONCLUSION

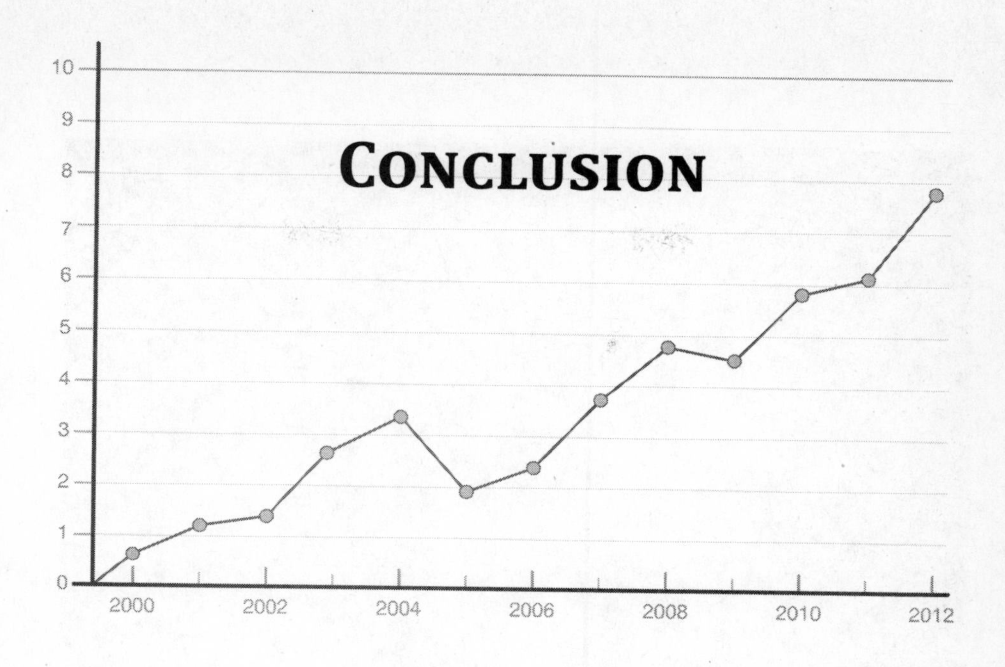

With the information contained in this book, you now have much better idea of what matters to your savings and can understand the intricacies of investing with not just diversification, which is fairly obvious to identify, but also with asset allocation, which provides further refinement to protect, preserve, and increase the value of your portfolio. You do not need to succumb to blindly following the advice of and trusting your financial adviser, and now, you can see the meaning behind the recommendations and question any that do not accord with your personal objectives.

Herald
NEW YORK
STREET
MONEY
Dow
5700
5650
5600

Appendix A: Risk Tolerance Questionnaire

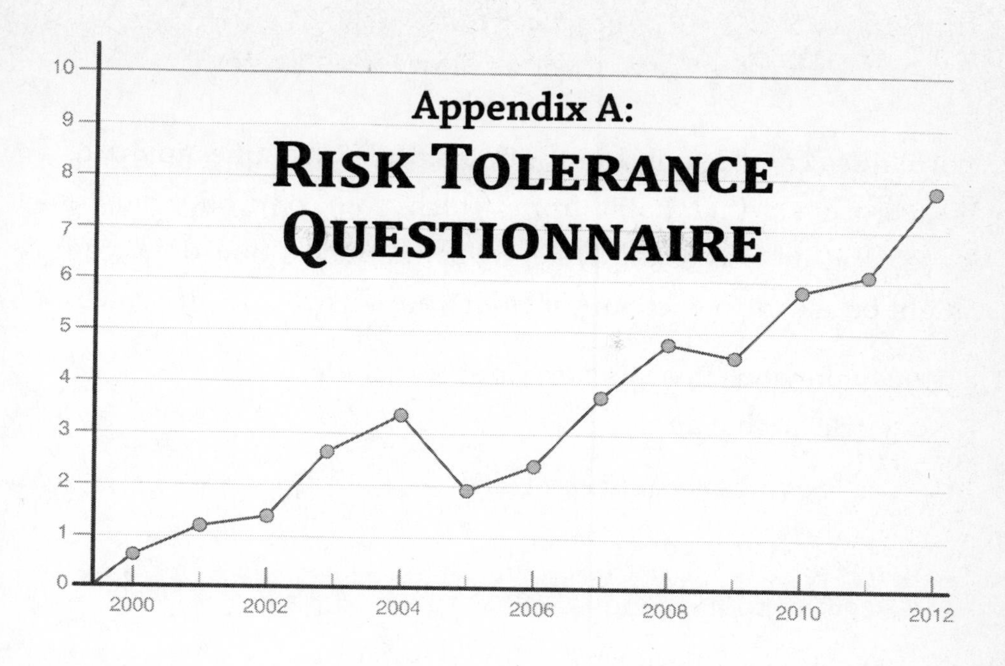

If you go to see investment advisor for help setting up your portfolio, you are likely to be asked to complete a risk questionnaire so the advisor can have an idea of your risk tolerance. The questionnaire sometimes will ask direct questions about hypothetical investments, and sometimes the questions are more general.

If you choose to complete a questionnaire for a specific brokerage or mutual fund company, expect some of the questions to be directed toward the company's products. The questions sometimes will even be phrased in such a way that they imply the products are best for your circumstances.

The way in which your financial advisor finds out about your preferences and risk tolerance should ultimately be in conversation with you because this is way the subtleties of your partialities can be found out. The risk tolerance questionnaire is a broad starting point from which your portfolio can be developed in discussion. Here are some typical questions you might be asked so you can consider your answers in advance.

1. My previous investing experience includes (circle all that apply):

    a. Savings accounts and CDs

    b. Treasury bonds

    c. Corporate bonds

    d. Mutual funds

    e. Large stocks

    f. Small-company stocks

    g. International stock investments

2. I intend to hold my investment portfolio for

    a. Up to two years

    b. Up to five years

    c. Up to 10 years

    d. More than 10 years

3. My reaction to inflation and my investment is

    a. I am happy if my investment keeps pace with inflation.

b. I would like my investment to grow faster than inflation.

c. I require my investment to achieve returns much greater than inflation.

4. You hold a major investment in an equity fund that loses 20 percent in a short time. How do you react?
   a. Sell your holding in the fund as quickly as possible.
   b. Sell half of your investment in the fund.
   c. Hold on to the investment with the hope the loss is a short-term fluctuation.
   d. Buy more of the fund to take advantage of the low price.

5. You hold a major investment in a mutual fund that has slowly lost value over a year and is now worth 20 percent less than it was a year ago. How do you react?
   a. Sell your holding in the fund.
   b. Sell half of your investment in the fund.
   c. Hold on to the investment and comfortably wait for the fund to recover.
   d. Buy more of the fund because it represents a bargain.
   e. Do nothing because you sold your interest in the fund once it started going down.

6. How do you feel about fluctuations in the value of your portfolio?

    a. I prefer little or no fluctuations in value even if it means lower returns.

    b. I will tolerate fluctuations up to 10 percent in the value for the opportunity to achieve favorable returns.

    c. I am not worried about large losses as long as my portfolio has a good chance of making high returns.

7. How stable are your current income sources?

    a. Steady, barring unforeseen circumstances

    b. Vary, according to how busy we are at work

    c. Fluctuate because I am self-employed

    d. Feast or famine; I get occasional big checks

Glossary of Terms

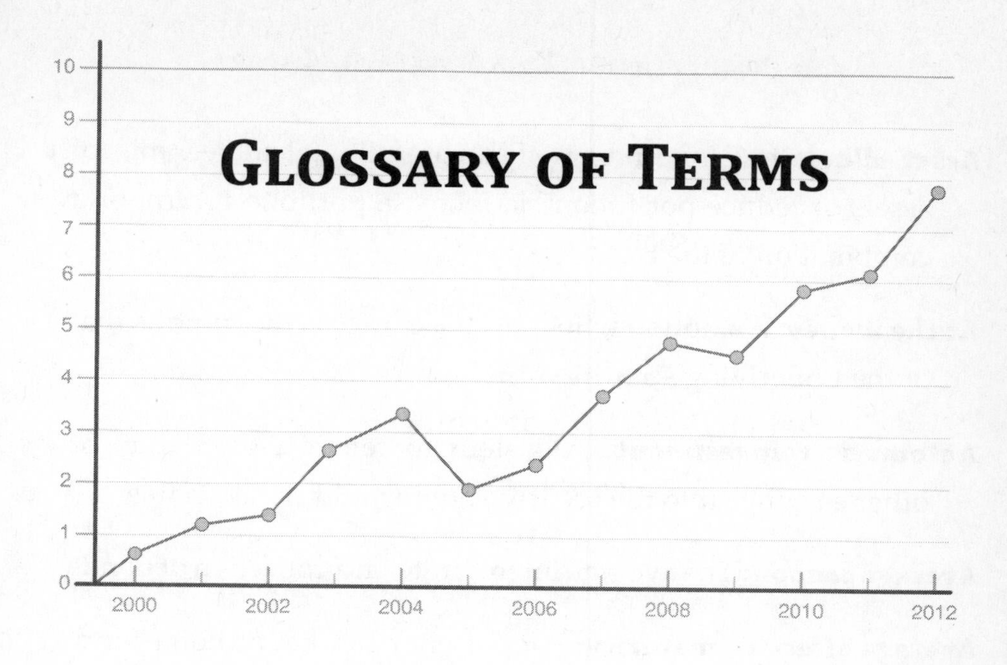

Accredited investor: Someone who is allowed by the Securities and Exchange Commission to invest in high risk investments because of their wealth

Active management: Active management is a strategy that plans to outperform the markets, by using the manager's judgment and experience

American Stock Exchange (AMEX): A stock exchange that specialized in small cap stocks and has merged with the NASDAQ

Arbitrage: Buying and selling something on different markets, to take advantage of a slight difference in pricing

Ask price: The price at which a security is offered for sale, sometimes called the offer

Asset allocation: Investing with a carefully calculated mix of assets to reduce portfolio risk, increase portfolio return, or a combination of the two

At the money: An option whose exercise price is the same as that of the underlying security

Automatic reinvestment: A system to reinvest dividends or other earnings into the security, buying additional shares

Average coupon: The average interest rate on a collection of bonds

Average effective maturity: For a money market or bond fund, this is the weighted average of the maturity dates; important because the longer it is to maturity, the more volatility in the fund

Back end load: The fee charged by some funds on selling the fund shares

Balance sheet: Summary of the company's financial position, including assets, liabilities, and shareholders' equity

Bankruptcy: Inability of a person or company to pay its debts

Basis point: Equal to one-hundredth of one percent and used to denote the change in a financial instrument

Bear market: A market where prices are going down

Below par: The price less than the face value of a security

Benchmark: A standard used to judge a fund manager's performance

Beta: A measure of risk in financial instruments

Bid price: The price the buyer is willing to pay for a security

Blue chip stocks: Common stocks of large well-known companies that have a history of good growth and dividends

Bonds: Financial instruments of debt

Bond fund: A fund that invests in bonds

Book value: The value of the company's assets, minus any liabilities

Broker: An individual or company that deals in the funds or other securities for the public

Bull market: A market where prices are rising in an uptrend

Call: An option that gives the right to buy a security at a certain price

Capital gains or losses: The difference between the selling price of an asset and the price originally paid

Capital gains distributions: These are payments to mutual fund shareholders of gains that the fund has realized in the year from sales at a profit, less any losses

Churning: Excessive trading in an account to generate more commissions for the broker

Close a position: To end a trade, usually by selling all the shares in a long position, or by "buying to cover" a short position

Closed end fund: A mutual fund with a fixed number of shares, usually listed on a stock exchange

Commodities: Large amounts of unprocessed goods, such as grains and metals, traded on the exchange

Contrarian: The trader who goes against the market

Correction: When a security dips in value temporarily from people taking profits

Correlation coefficient: A number between -1 and 1 which gives a relationship between the movement of two securities' prices

Cost basis: The original cost of an investment

Coupon: The interest rate paid on the bond until maturity

Currency risk: In a global investing, the chance that currency exchange rates will vary to the detriment of the investor

Depression: A long-term decline in the economy

Derivative: A type of investment whose value is derived from an underlying security

Discount broker: A brokerage firm that executes orders at a low rate of commission

Discount rate: The interest rate that the Federal Reserve charges a bank to borrow funds

Diversification: Investing in different market sectors to avoid any particular market weakness affecting the whole portfolio

Dividend: May be paid to stockholders from company profits

Dividend reinvestment plan: A system to automatically reinvest any dividends paid back into the security, buying more shares

Dollar cost averaging: The system of investing in securities with a regular fixed payment, which averages the price paid

Earnings: The net income of a company

Earnings per share: Total earnings for the company divided by the number of shares outstanding

EBIDTA: Company earnings before interest, debt, taxes, and amortization

Efficient frontier: The efficient frontier is a line chart that represents the best possible combination of risk and return

Emerging-market fund: A fund that invests in a growing market

Equity: A stock, or the value of securities in a brokerage account

Exchange traded fund (ETF): The fund, usually a simple index fund, which trades on an exchange. Unlike a mutual fund, the value is not fixed by the holdings, but varies with supply and demand on the exchange

Expense ratio: The percentage of the fund's assets used to meet expenses, such as management and office fees

FDIC: The Federal Deposit Insurance Corporation, which promotes confidence in banks by insuring deposits against bank failure

Federal Reserve Board: An agency responsible for setting fiscal policy by regulating the discount rate

Fee only adviser: A financial advisor who charges a set rate, rather than receiving income from commission on products traded

Fixed income: Income from a financial instrument paying a fixed rate, such as bonds

Front end load: A sales fee charged at the time of buying some funds – cf back end load

Fund: Organized by a financial company, an investment organization in which you can buy shares

Fund of funds: A fund that invests in other mutual funds

Fundamental analysis: Examining the true worth of a company, in terms of its assets, sales, expenses, etc., in order to assess the long-term value of the shares

Futures: Contracts to buy or sell specific amounts and types of commodity at an agreed price on a certain future date

Futures option: An option to buy or sell a futures contract

Global fund: A mutual fund that invests in shares from around the world

Gross Domestic Product (GDP): The output of the nation generated within the countries boundaries

Growth fund: A fund that specifically seeks capital gain in choosing investments

Hedge: A financial strategy to offset potential losses in one security against another

Hedge fund: An investment fund that is able to use many strategies, including derivatives and short selling, to optimize returns

In the money: An option that will make a profit if exercised

Intrinsic value: The amount by which an option is in the money

Index: A measure of the value of shares in a market, such as the Dow Jones Industrial Average, the S&P 500, the NASDAQ, the FTSE 100, etc.

Index fund: A mutual fund or exchange traded funds designed to mimic the value of a stock market index

Inflation risk: The risk that inflation will reduce or make negative the returns on a particular investment

Interest rate risk: The risk that the value of a bond will decline because of a rise in general interest rates

International fund: A mutual fund that invests in shares from outside the United States

Investment advisor: A person qualified by experience and examination to assist in investment decisions

Investment Advisers Act: A law passed in 1940 that governs the actions of investment advisers

Junk bonds: A bond with a low credit rating, and a compensatory high yield for those prepared to take the risk

Large cap: One of the companies with the largest capitalization

Life-cycle fund: A fund in which investments are changed over time to suit an anticipated date for redemption

Liquidate: Converting assets into cash

Liquidity: A measure of how quickly a security can be sold for a fair price

Load: A sales charge

Load fund: A mutual fund that has a sales charge

Long: Holding financial securities in order to profit if the price increases

Long-Term Equity Anticipation Securities (LEAPS): Publicly traded options contracts that have an expiration longer than one year

Low load fund: A mutual fund that charges 3 ½ percent or less as its load

Management fee: The amount paid to the investment advisor

Margin: The amount borrowed from a broker in a margin account

Margin call: Notification from your broker that additional funds are required to cover your losses

Market capitalization: The value of the company; the share price times the number of shares outstanding

Master fund: A fund that invests in other funds

Maturity: The date when the principal is to be paid back on a bond

Mid cap: A large company, but smaller than the large-cap companies; different markets set different levels of capitalization

Money market: Lending or borrowing funds for less than three years

Money market fund: A fund that invests in short-term securities

Municipal bond: A government issued bond

Mutual fund: An investment fund operated by a company

National Association of Security Dealers (NASD): A self-regulatory organization of the securities industry responsible for the operation and regulation of the NASDAQ stock market and over-the-counter markets; also administrated exams for investment professionals, such as the Series 7 exam

Negative correlation: Two securities have negative correlation if their values move in opposite directions

Net asset value (NAV): The value of a mutual fund holding, calculated from the securities held less liabilities, divided by the number of fund shares outstanding

Net worth: The total value of all assets and possessions minus the total of liabilities and debts

No load fund: A mutual fund that has no sales charges or commissions

Nominal return: The way most returns are quoted; the nominal return does not make allowance for inflation

New York Stock Exchange (NYSE): A stock exchange located in lower Manhattan, New York City; is the world's largest stock exchange

Open end fund: A fund without limitation on issuing or redeeming shares

Open interest: The number of derivatives contracts that have not been exercised offset

Operating expenses: The costs associated with running a fund, which includes management fees and expenses

Option: A contract with the right but not the obligation to buy or sell securities at a certain price on or before a set date

Out of the money: An option contract where the underlying security is worth less than the strike price

Paper loss: A loss in a security that has yet to be sold

Par: The face value of a security

Perfect negative correlation: Two investments whose returns fluctuate in the opposite direction to each other

Portfolio: A collection of equities, bonds, and other financial instruments held by an individual or by a company

Positive correlation: Two securities have positive correlation if their values move together

Premium: Amount by which the price of the security exceeds the face value; also the amount paid to buy an option contract

Price to earnings ratio (P/E): The stock price divided by the per-share earnings for the last year; commonly used as a guide to whether a stock is over or under valued

Prospectus: A document that describes the investment, such as a mutual fund, to potential shareholders

Puts: An option that gives the right to sell a security at a predetermined price at a future date

Real estate investment trust (REIT): The company that manages a group of real estate investments and in which you can buy shares

Real return: The real return is the return after adjustment for inflation

Rebalancing: The process of restoring the target allocations of different types of securities in your portfolio

Recession: A downturn in the economy that is defined as a drop in Gross National Product for two successive quarters

REITs: Real estate investment trusts; companies that earn income from rental or mortgages of properties

Risk tolerance: An investor's willingness to tolerate the ups and downs of a security's price

ROI: Return on investment, or income divided by the investment

Sales charge: Otherwise known as load; a charge to investors for buying or redeeming their shares in a fund

Sector fund: A mutual fund that specializes in investing in a particular market sector

Securities and Exchange Commission (SEC): The government agency that regulates much of investment, including the markets, funds, financial advisors, and brokers

Shares: Ownership in a company

Shareholders: Shareholders buy shares in a company and own (a part of) the company; they can vote, at least annually, on company policies and appoint the Board of Directors

Short sale: For stocks, the sale of securities that are not owned, borrowed by the broker on your behalf, in the expectation that they will fall in value and can be replaced more cheaply

Small cap: Companies that are less capitalized than mid-cap

Standard & Poor's (S&P): A company that rates stocks, bonds, and credit, and issues indices of values

Standard deviation: Standard deviation is a measure of investment volatility, or how much it varies over time

Stock: Ownership of part of a company

Stop loss order: An order to your broker to sell a stock if it falls to a certain price level

Strike price: The price per share of the security that is the subject of an option

Tax-exempt bond: Usually issued by a municipality or government agency; a bond which has tax advantages on the gains

Tax-free fund: A fund that makes investments that are not taxable

Total return: The total return is the combination of growth in value and the income or dividend

Treasury bill: U.S. debt obligation with a maturity date less than one year

Treasury bond: U.S. debt obligation with a maturity date of ten or more years

Treasury note: U.S. debt obligation with a maturity date from one year to ten years

Trend: The direction of the market

Volatility: The amount of fluctuation in the price of a security; sometimes expressed mathematically as for example "standard deviation"

Wall Street: The physical home of the NYSE and many financial companies

BIBLIOGRAPHY

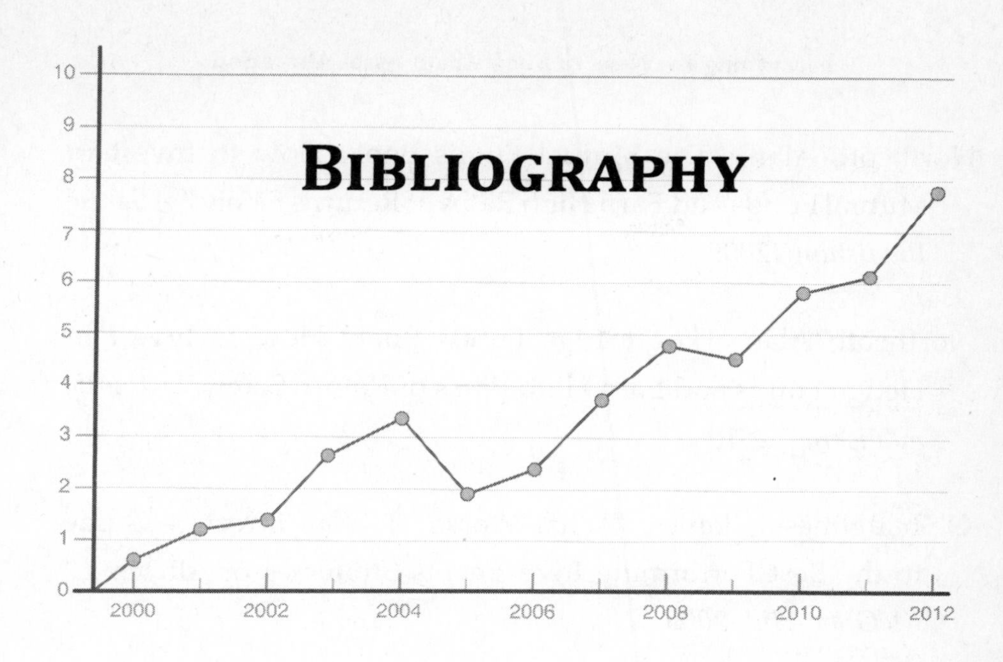

Darst, David M., "The Art of Asset Allocation," *McGraw-Hill, 2008*

Ferri, Richard A., "All about Asset Allocation," *McGraw-Hill, 2006*

Gibson, Roger C., "Asset Allocation Balancing Financial Risk," *McGraw-Hill, 2008*

Miccolis, Jerry A. & Perrucci, Dorianne R., "Asset Allocation for Dummies," *Wiley Publishing, 2009*

Picerno, James, "Dynamic Asset Allocation," *Bloomberg Press, 2010*

Kiyosaki, Robert T., "Rich Dad's Guide to Investing," *Warner Business Books, 2000*

Northcott, Alan, "The Mutual Funds Book: How to Invest in Mutual Funds and Earn High Rates of Returns Safely," *Atlantic Publishing, 2009*

Northcott, Alan, "The Hedge Funds Book: How to Invest in Hedge Funds and Earn High Rates of Return Safely," *Atlantic publishing, 2010*

O'Shaughnessy, James, "What Works on Wall Street: a Guide to the Best Performing Investments Strategies of All Time," *McGraw-Hill, 2005*

AUTHOR BIOGRAPHY

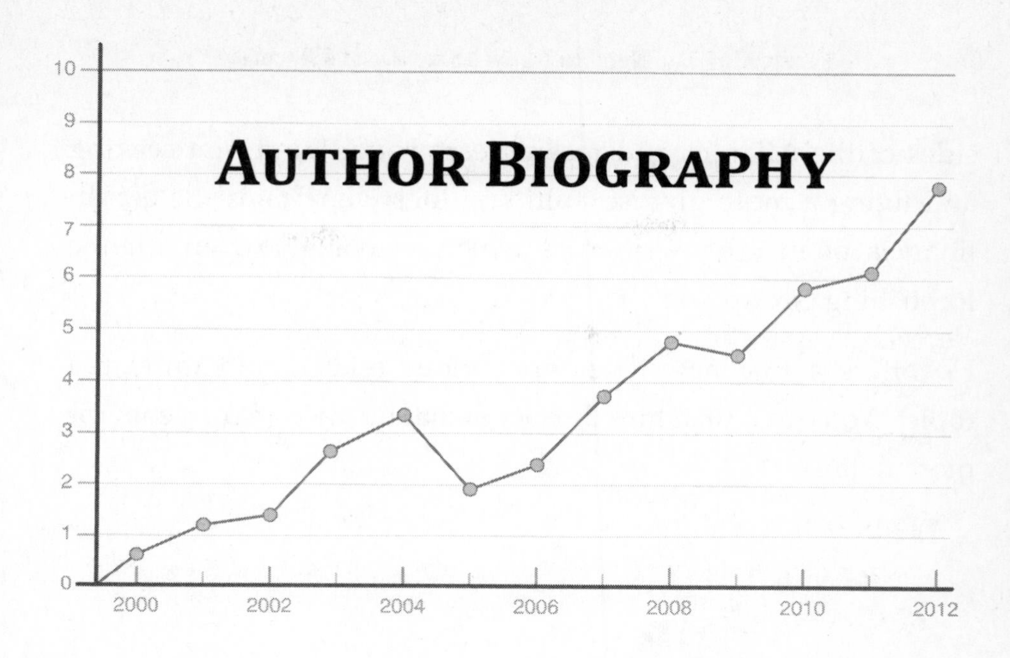

Alan Northcott is a successful financial author, freelance writer, trading educator, professional engineer, radio broadcaster, farmer, karaoke jockey, and wedding officiant along with other pursuits. He and his wife live in Colorado where they share their house with many dogs and cats. They have three children living on three different continents and two grandchildren, one of whom, thankfully, also lives in Colorado, which allows them to see him grow up.

Originating from England, he was educated at Eltham College in London and obtained his degree from the University of Surrey, also in England. He immigrated with his wife to America in 1992. His engineering career spanned more than 30 years on both sides of the Atlantic, and recent years have found him seeking and living a more diverse, fulfilling lifestyle. This is the eighth financial book he has written, all which are available from Atlantic Publishing Group, Inc.

He offers a free newsletter on various related and unrelated topics. You can e-mail him directly at alannorthcott@msn.com for more details.

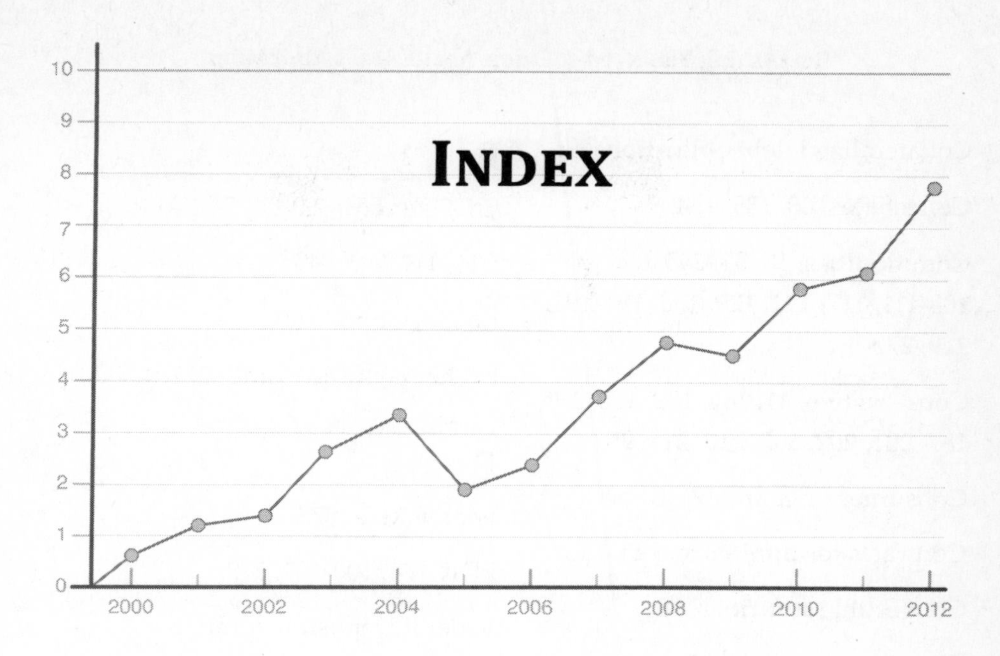

Index

D

E

F

G

H

I

J

K

M

N

O

P